No Nonsense Number

Activities to support the teaching of
number knowledge, addition and subtraction,
multiplication and fractions
Key Stage 1 objectives for older pupils
Book 2

Suzi de Gouveia, Jackie Andrews
and Jude Callaghan

essential resources

Title:	No Nonsense Number Activities to support the teaching of number knowledge, addition, subtraction, multiplication and fractions – Key Stage 1 objectives for older pupils Book 2
Authors:	Suzi de Gouveia, Jackie Andrews and Jude Callaghan
Editor:	Tanya Tremewan
Book code:	393B
ISBN:	978-1-877523-25-0
Published:	2009
Publisher:	Essential Resources Educational Publishers Limited

United Kingdom:	**Australia:**	**New Zealand:**
Unit 8–10 Parkside	PO Box 90	PO Box 5036
Shortgate Lane	Oak Flats,	Invercargill
Laughton, BN8 6DG	NSW 2529	
ph: 0845 3636 147	ph: 1800 005 068	ph: 0800 087 376
fax: 0845 3636 148	fax: 1800 981 213	fax: 0800 937 825

Website:	www.essentialresourcesuk.com
Copyright:	Text: © Suzi de Gouveia, Jackie Andrews and Jude Callaghan, 2009 Edition and Illustrations: © Essential Resources Educational Publishers Limited, 2009
About the authors:	Suzi is the enthusiastic headteacher of St Teresa's Primary School in Christchurch, New Zealand. She has international teaching experience and has had the pleasure of teaching in a multi-cultural environment. Over 20 years of teaching have enabled Suzi to develop a wealth of ideas and resources to best help children in their learning. Jackie is an experienced teacher who has taught primary school children in both New Zealand and the United Kingdom. As a mother of four young children she is beginning to wonder where the time to diversify has gone. Jude is an experienced, enthusiastic teacher with a passion for teaching and learning. Her teaching programmes are innovative and exciting. She has joined the writing team to share her deep understanding and wealth of ideas.

Photocopy Notice:

Permission is given to schools and teachers who buy this book to reproduce it (and/or any extracts) by photocopying or otherwise, but only for use at their present school. Copies may not be supplied to anyone else or made or used for any other purpose.

Contents

Introduction 4
Curriculum links 4

Activity sheets
Recognising the number before and after 5
Working with 5: patterns and groups 14
Solving addition problems by counting 22
Adding and taking away 1 24
Solving subtraction problems by counting 30
Recalling addition and subtraction facts 32
Counting in twos and fives 34
Showing and finding half 38

Activity cards
Overview 43
Monster hands and feet 44
Before and after 46
Before and after bingo 47
Addition and subtraction carrots 48
Make it 50

Introduction

This book is one of a number in the *No Nonsense Number* series aimed at older children who are still working towards Key Stage 1 learning objectives in maths.

This book contains two sections. The first section comprises **activity sheets** to support the learning and consolidation of concepts at this key stage.

The second section is comprised of **activity cards**. These templates can be used in a variety of ways to develop number knowledge through independent, individual and group work.

Children who are having difficulty grasping concepts benefit from repetitive activities. For this reason, games – which offer a variety of repetitive elements – have been included in both sections of this book. In the activity sheets section, children can make the games themselves to play either in class or at home.

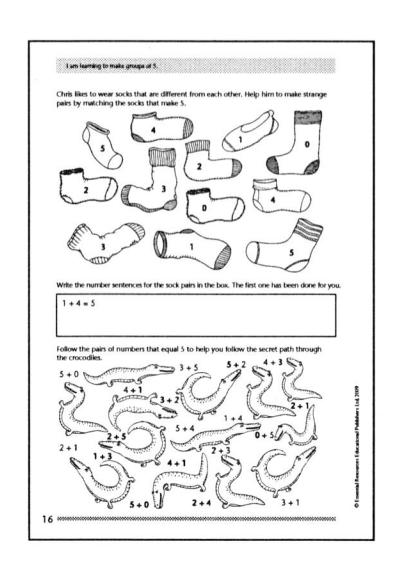

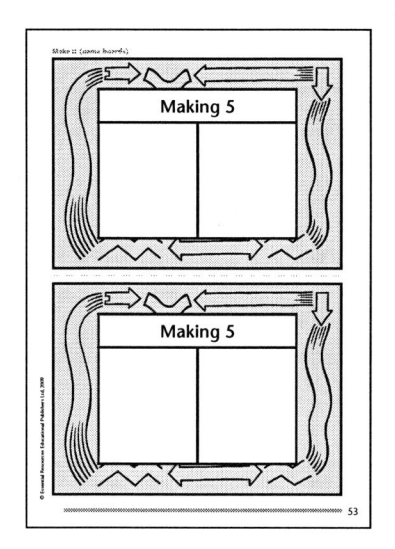

Curriculum links

Strand	Objective(s) *Most children learn to:*
Year 1	
Using and applying mathematics	• solve problems involving counting, adding, subtracting, doubling or halving in the context of numbers, measures or money, for example to "pay" and "give change
Counting and understanding number	• say the number that is 1 more or less than any given number • use the vocabulary of halves in context
Knowing and using number facts	• derive and recall all pairs of numbers with a total of 10 and addition facts for totals to at least 5; work out the corresponding subtraction facts • count on or back in ones, two and fives
Calculating	• relate addition to counting on; use practical and informal written methods to support the addition of a one-digit number to a one-digit number • understand subtraction as "take away"; use practical and informal written methods to support the subtraction of a one-digit number from a one-digit or two-digit number • use the vocabulary related to addition and subtraction and symbols to describe and record addition and subtraction number sentences

Source: Adapted from Primary Framework for Literacy and Mathematics, 2006

Recognising the number before and after

I am learning to recognise the number before and the number after up to 10.

Make each item a pound **more**. Cross out the amount on the price tag and write in the new amount.

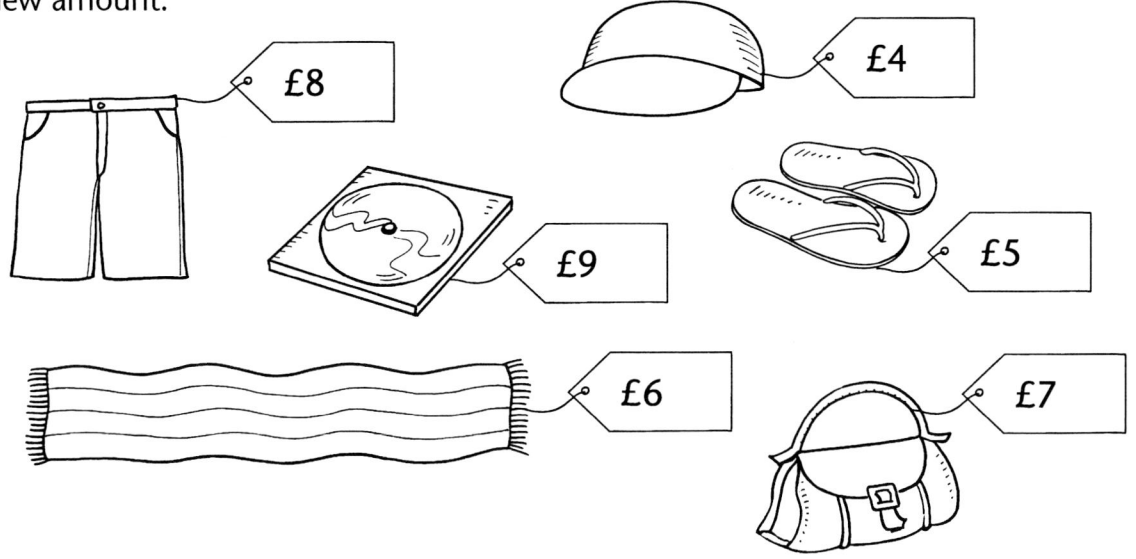

£8   £4   £9   £5   £6   £7

Make each item a pound **less**. Cross out the amount on the price tag and write in the new amount.

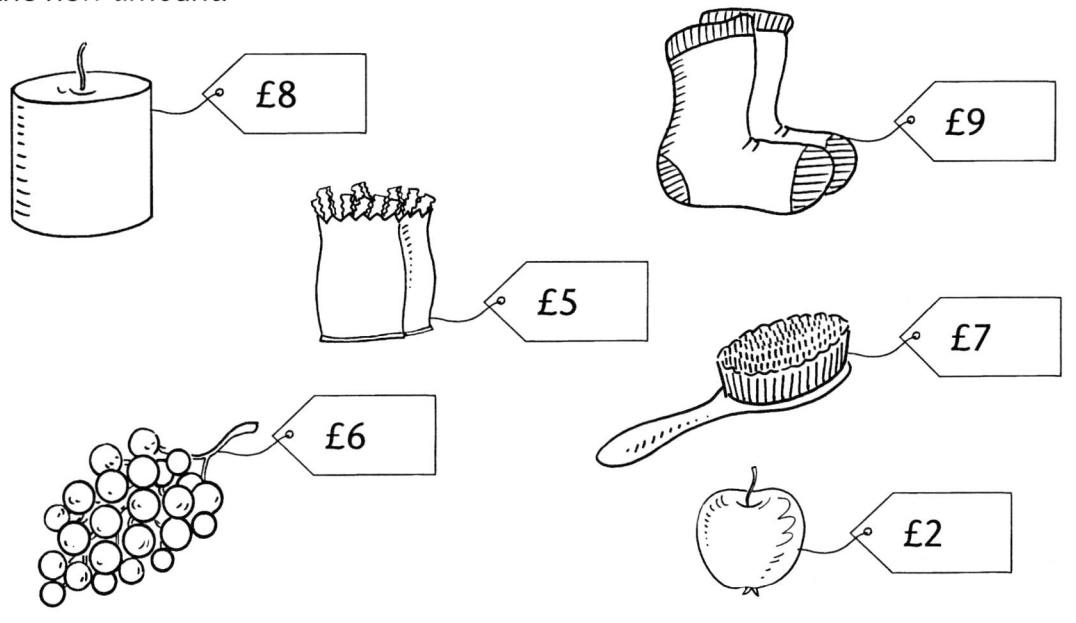

£8   £9   £5   £7   £6   £2

Make each of these numbers one **more**.

5		9	
7		4	
3		6	
8		2	

Make each of these numbers one **less**.

4		10	
9		7	
6		8	
3		5	

I am learning the number before and the number after up to 10.

These teams brought oranges to their game. Give each team **one more** point for being helpful.

Bulldogs	3	
Rabbits	7	
Cheetahs	5	
Lions	2	
Hippos	9	

Flames	1	
Sting	8	
Rebels	0	
Diamonds	6	
Force	4	

These teams didn't wear the correct uniforms. Take **one point** off each team.

Wizards	4	
Knights	10	
Volts	8	
Blues	3	
Giants	6	

Warriors	1	
Highlanders	5	
Stags	9	
Chiefs	2	
Tornadoes	7	

The number machine is broken. It should show the number before or the number after. Help fix it by filling in the missing numbers.

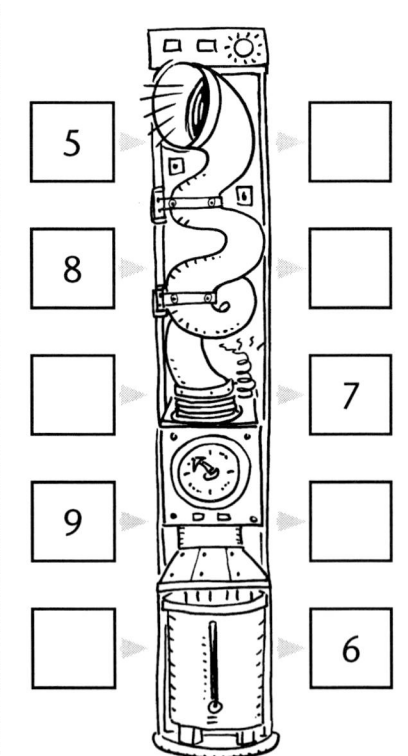

5 ▸ ☐
8 ▸ ☐
☐ ▸ 7
9 ▸ ☐
☐ ▸ 6

I am learning to recognise the number before and the number after up to 10.

Fill in the missing number on each monster's hand or foot. The first one has been done for you.

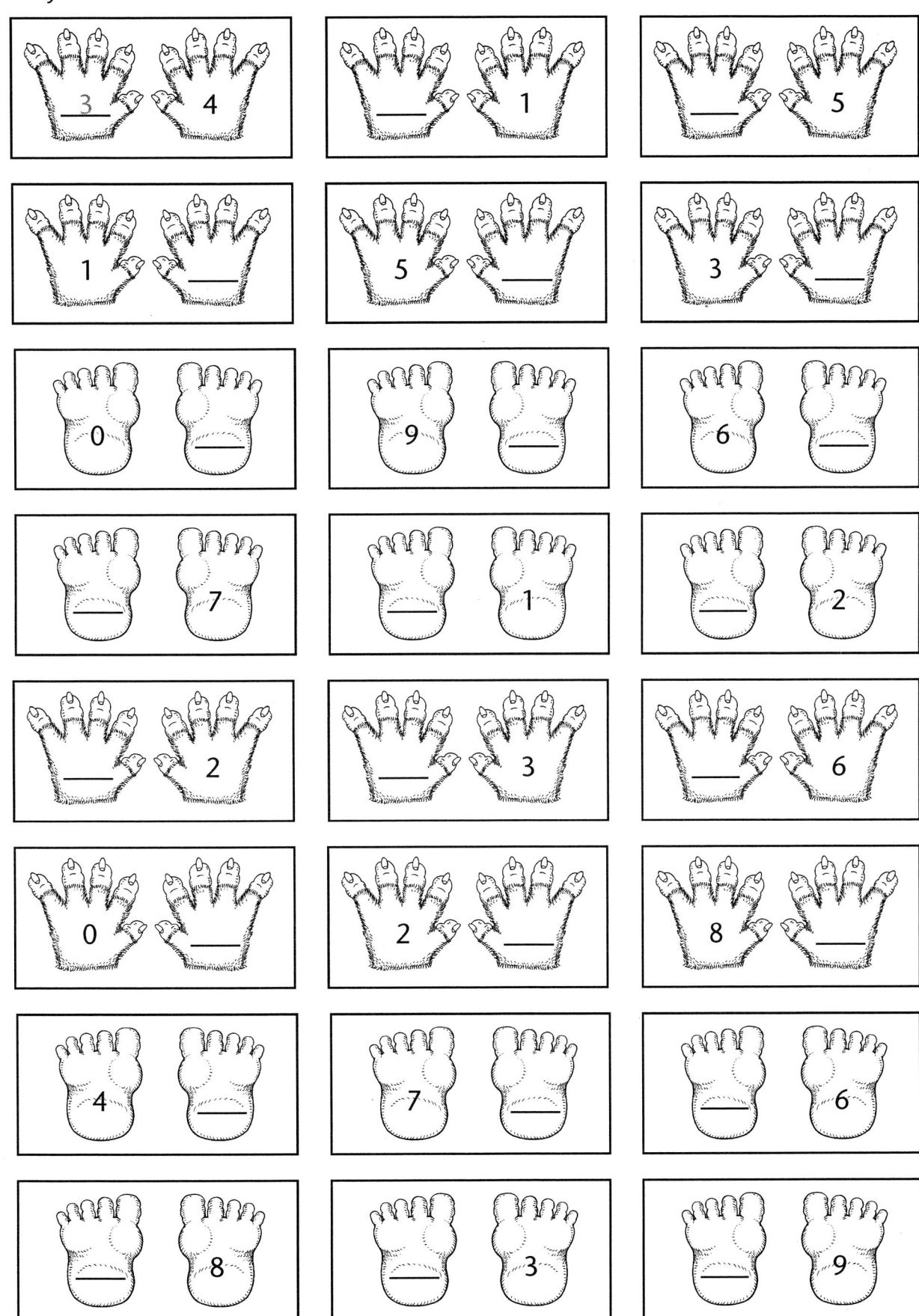

3 , 4	___ , 1	___ , 5
1 , ___	5 , ___	3 , ___
0 , ___	9 , ___	6 , ___
___ , 7	___ , 1	___ , 2
___ , 2	___ , 3	___ , 6
0 , ___	2 , ___	8 , ___
4 , ___	7 , ___	___ , 6
___ , 8	___ , 3	___ , 9

I am learning to recognise the number before and the number after up to 20.

Fill in the missing number on each monster's hand or foot. The first one has been done for you.

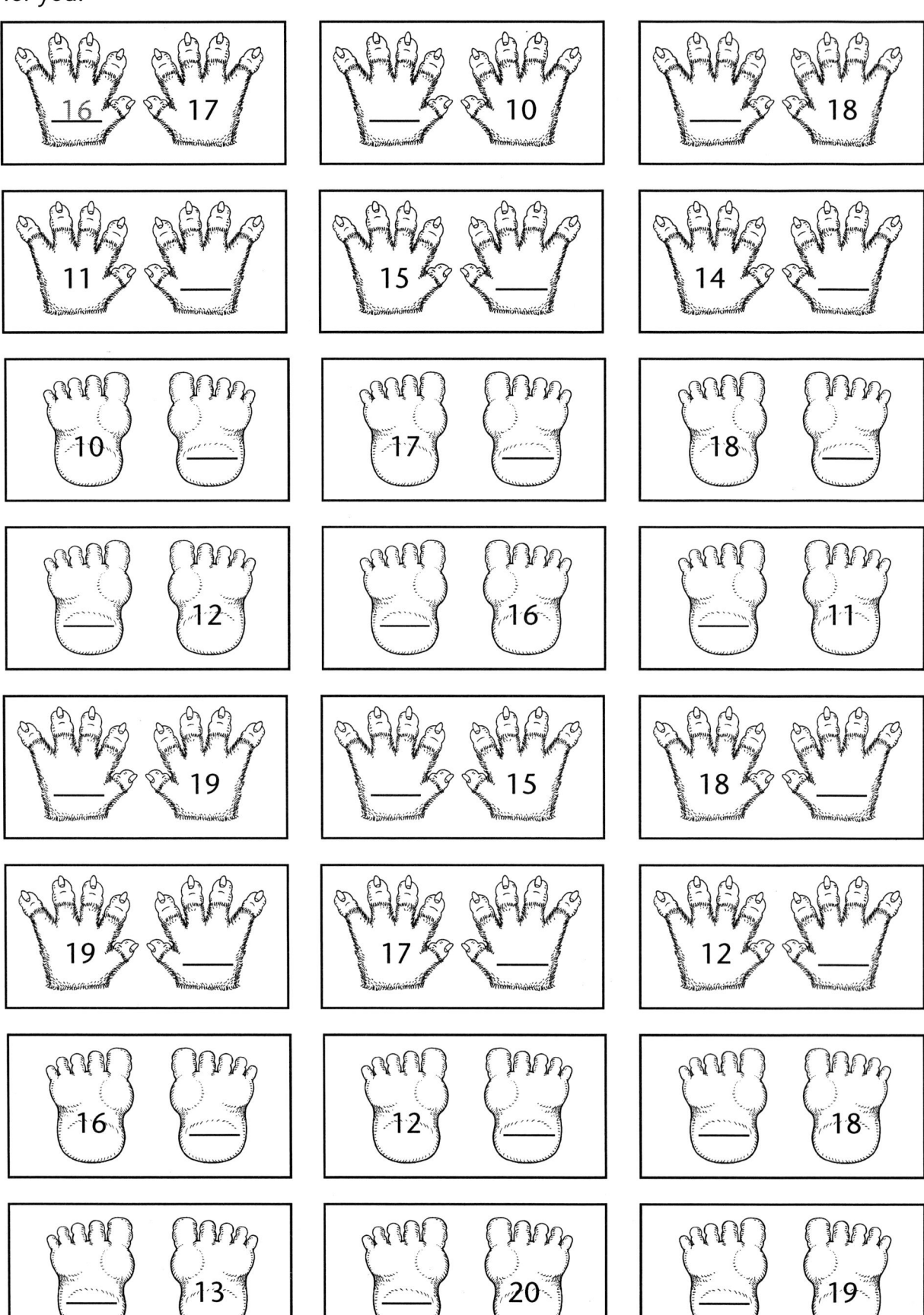

16, 17	___, 10	___, 18
11, ___	15, ___	14, ___
10, ___	17, ___	18, ___
___, 12	___, 16	___, 11
___, 19	___, 15	18, ___
19, ___	17, ___	12, ___
16, ___	12, ___	___, 18
___, 13	___, 20	___, 19

I am learning to recognise the number before and the number after up to 20.

Make each item a pound **more**. Cross out the amount on the price tag and write in the new amount.

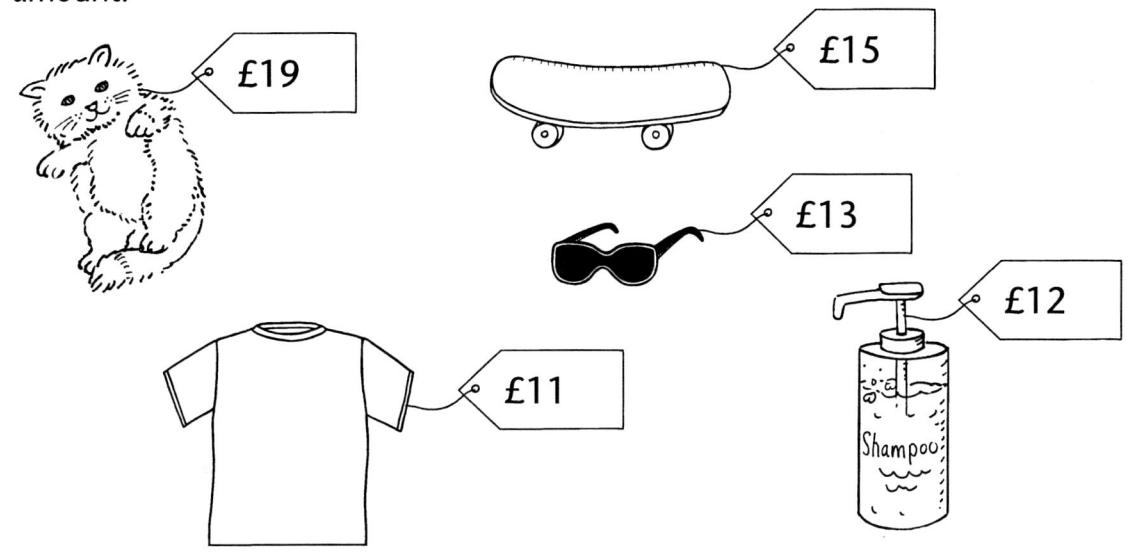

£19

£15

£13

£12

£11

Make each item a pound **less**. Cross out the amount on the price tag and write in the new amount.

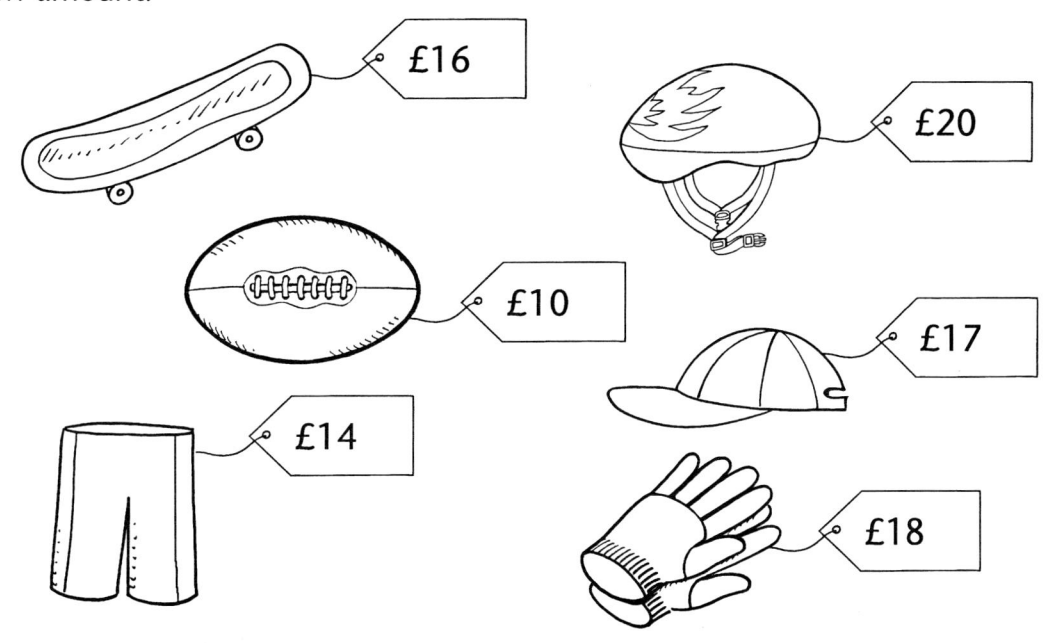

£16

£20

£10

£17

£14

£18

Make each of these numbers one **more**.

12	
18	
19	
17	

10	
14	
16	
13	

Make each of these numbers one **less**.

11	
13	
16	
15	

19	
14	
12	
17	

9

I am learning the number before and the number after up to 20.

Throughout the season, these teams displayed fair play.
Give each team one more point for being good sports.

Bulldogs	12	
Rabbits	16	
Cheetahs	10	
Lions	18	
Hippos	14	

Flames	19	
Sting	15	
Rebels	11	
Diamonds	17	
Force	13	

These teams argued with the referee. Take one point off each team.

Wizards	20	
Knights	17	
Volts	12	
Blues	18	
Giants	14	

Warriors	16	
Highlanders	11	
Stags	15	
Chiefs	13	
Tornadoes	19	

The number machine is broken. It should show the number before or the number after. Help fix it by filling in the missing numbers.

11 → □
15 → □
□ → 12
16 → □
□ → 19

I am learning to recognise the number before and the number after up to 20.

Choose the number that comes **before** and the number that comes **after** to fill in the spaces on the bricks.

	15				11				17	
12	14	17	16	10	18	12	14	19	15	18	16

	6				10				5	
7	8	4	5	12	9	5	11	6	7	3	4

	4				11				14	
5	6	2	3	13	12	9	10	11	13	16	15

	7				14				12	
8	9	6	5	15	11	16	13	10	14	11	13

	9				19				3	
8	7	11	10	17	18	16	20	2	6	1	4

	15				8				16	
16	17	14	13	5	7	10	9	13	17	18	15

	13				2				12	
12	16	14	10	5	0	1	3	16	11	14	13

	1				13				18	
3	5	0	2	12	15	14	16	16	17	20	19

I am learning the number before and the number after up to 20.

Link the number in the grey box to the number that comes **before** and the number that comes **after** it. The first one has been started for you.

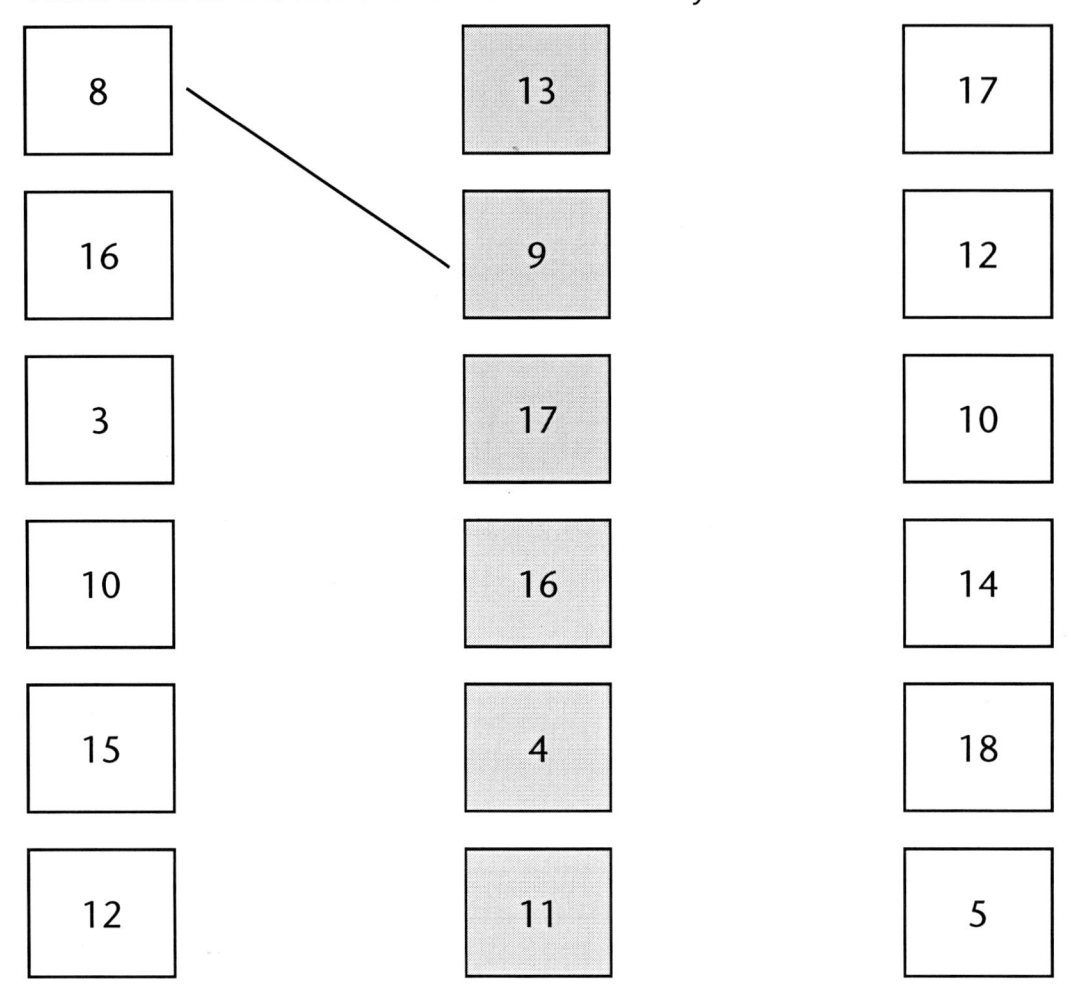

8	13	17
16	9	12
3	17	10
10	16	14
15	4	18
12	11	5

Write the number that comes **after** the number shown on the jigsaw puzzle.

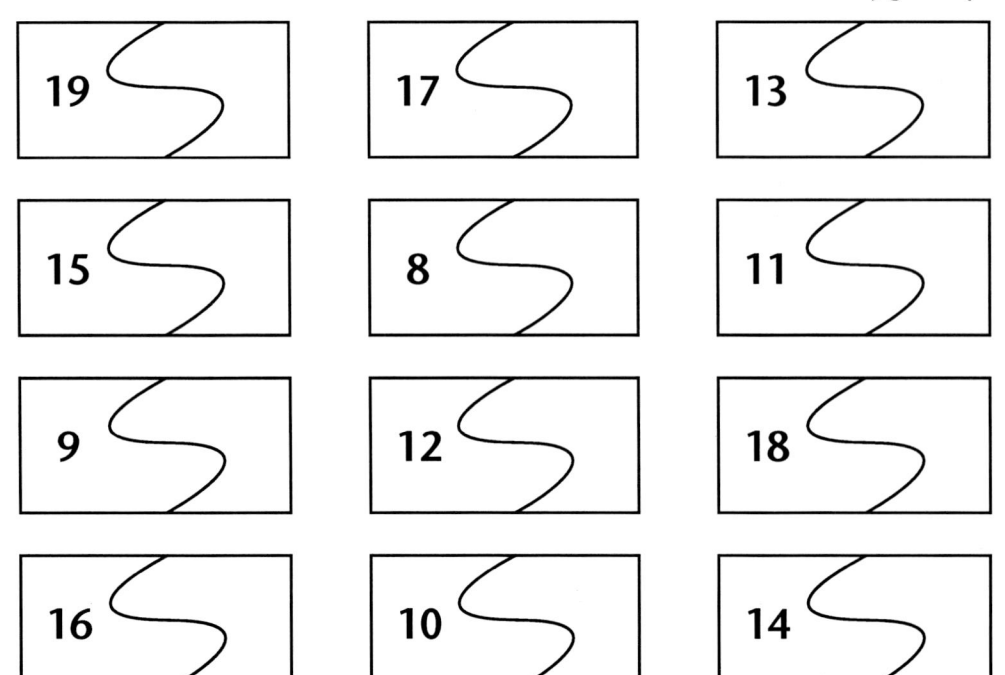

19   17   13

15   8   11

9   12   18

16   10   14

I am learning to recognise the number before and the number after up to 20.

Write the number that comes **before** each of these numbers.

	12			6			17
	3			11			15
	16			13			20
	10			7			5

Write the number that comes **after** each of these numbers.

13			7			19	
8			14			10	
15			9			12	
6			5			18	

Write the number that comes **between** each pair of numbers.

9		11		18		20
1		3		9		11
7		9		16		18
13		15		8		10
3		5		12		14

Working with 5: patterns and groups

I am learning to recognise patterns within 5.

For each cake, count the number of candles that are glowing and write the number in the box for glowing candles. Then count the number that have been blown out and write the number in the box for candles that have been blown out.

See how quickly you can fill in the missing numbers to make these number sentences correct.

____ + 4 = 5   2 + ____ = 5   ____ + 5 = 5

5 + ____ = 5   1 + ____ = 5   ____ + 2 = 5

3 + ____ = 5   4 + ____ = 5   0 + ____ = 5

5 = ____ + 1   ____ + 3 = 5   ____ + 1 = 5

5 = 5 + ____   5 = 0 + ____   5 = ____ + 2

5 = 1 + ____   5 = ____ + 3   5 = 4 + ____

5 = 3 + ____   5 = 2 + ____   5 = ____ + 5

Draw the other hand with the finger pattern needed to make 5.

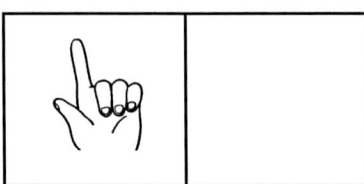

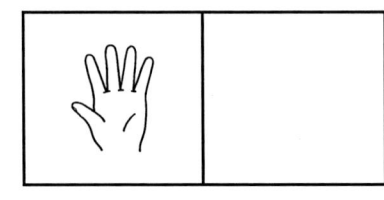

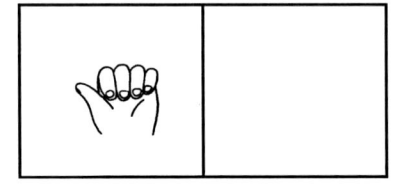

14

I am learning to recognise number patterns within 5.

Make each domino add up to 5 and fill in blanks in its number sentence.

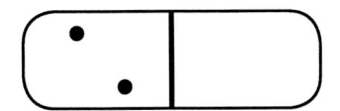

___ + ___ = 5 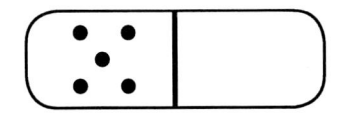   ___ + ___ = 5 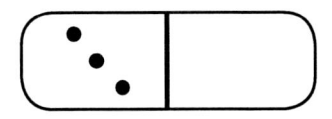   ___ + ___ = 5

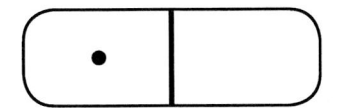

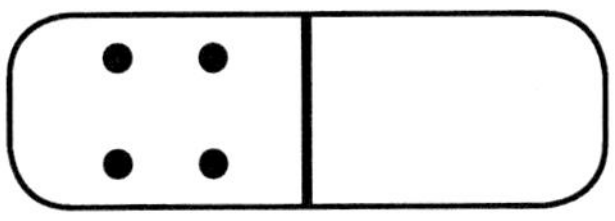

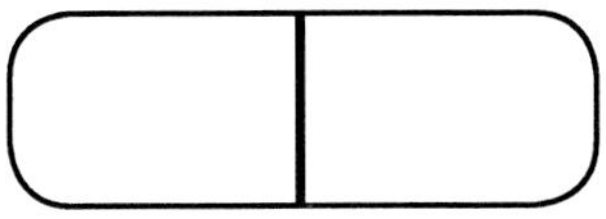

___ + ___ = ___   ___ + ___ = ___   0 + ___ = ___

Now make your own dominoes to add up to 5 and fill in the blanks.

___ + ___ = ___   ___ + ___ = ___   ___ + ___ = ___

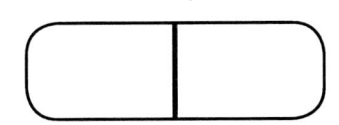

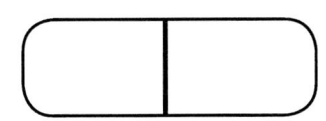

Make each tens frame show 5. Then complete the number sentences. The first one has been started for you.

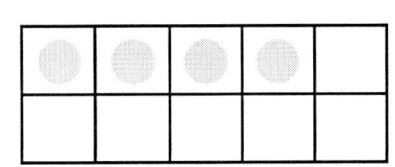

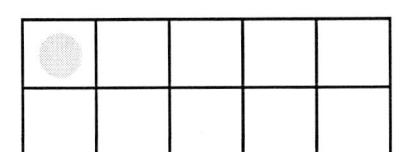

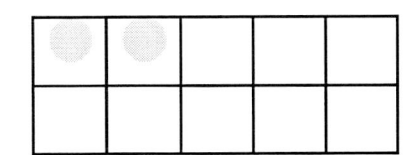

_1_ and ___ makes 5.   ___ and ___ makes 5.

_1_ + ___ = 5   ___ + ___ = 5

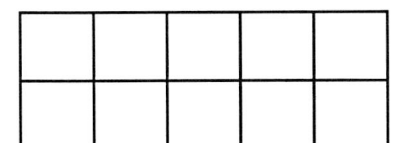

___ and ___ makes 5.   ___ and ___ makes 5.

___ + ___ = 5   ___ + ___ = 5

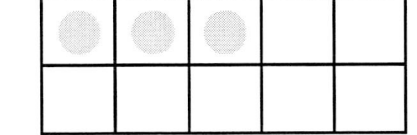

___ and ___ makes 5.   ___ and ___ makes 5.

___ + ___ = 5   ___ + ___ = 5

I am learning to make groups of 5.

Chris likes to wear socks that are different from each other. Help him to make strange pairs by matching the socks that make 5.

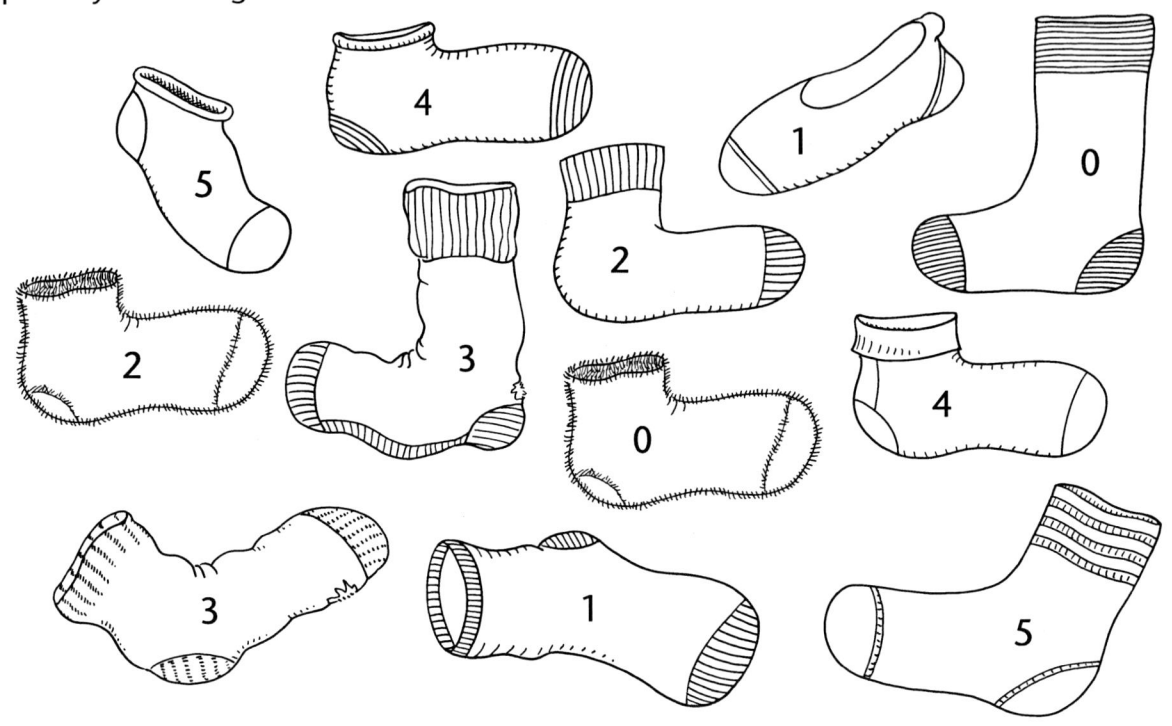

Write the number sentences for the sock pairs in the box. The first one has been done for you.

1 + 4 = 5

Follow the pairs of numbers that equal 5 to help you follow the secret path through the crocodiles.

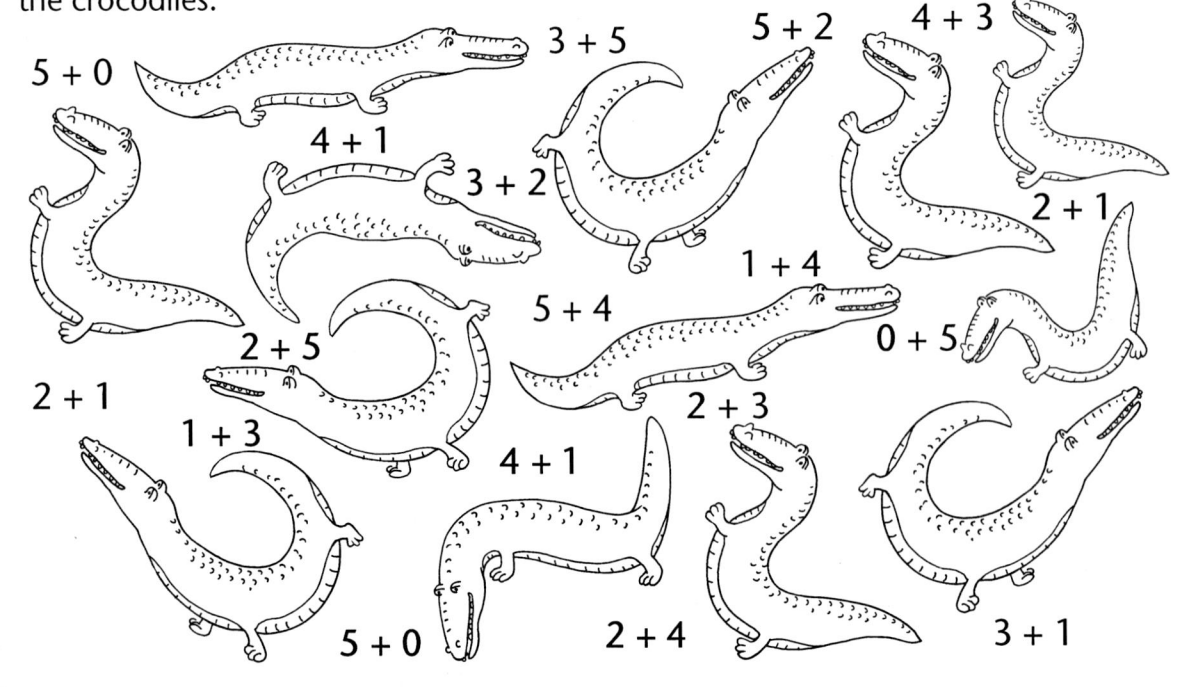

5 + 0   3 + 5   5 + 2   4 + 3
4 + 1   3 + 2   2 + 1
2 + 5   5 + 4   1 + 4
2 + 1   1 + 3   4 + 1   2 + 3   0 + 5
        5 + 0   2 + 4   3 + 1

16

I am learning to make groups of five.

Make each set up to five. Write the number sentence for each one. The first one has been started for you.

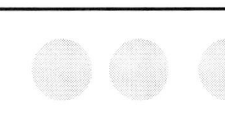

 _4_ + ___ = _5_

___ + ___ = ___

___ + ___ = ___

___ + ___ = ___

___ + ___ = ___

___ + ___ = ___

5 = ___ + ___

5 = ___ + ___

5 = ___ + ___

5 = ___ + ___

5 = ___ + ___

5 = ___ + ___

Complete these number sentences using your answers from the boxes above.

5 = ___ + 2   1 + ___ = 5   5 = 0 + ___

3 + 2 = ___   5 = 4 + ___   5 + ___ = 5

17

I am learning to recognise patterns within 5.

Cut out the finger patterns from the bottom of the page. Stick each one in the correct place. Then complete the number sentence.

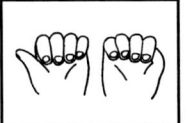

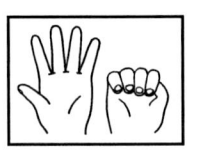

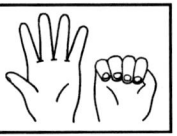

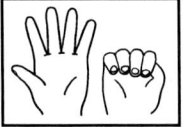

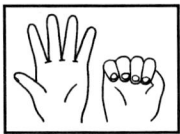

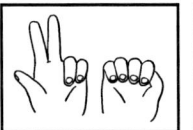

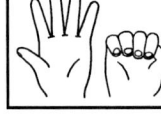

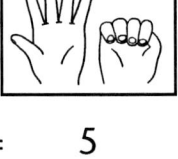

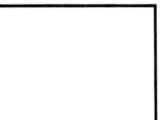

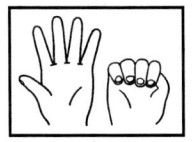

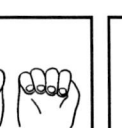

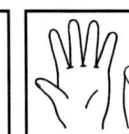

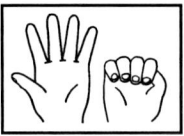

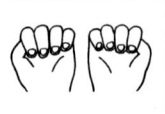

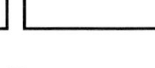

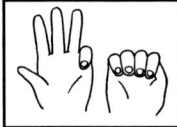

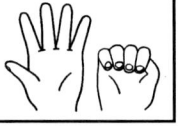

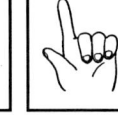

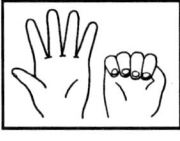

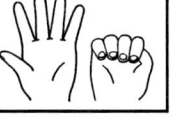

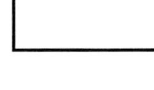

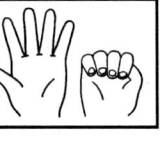

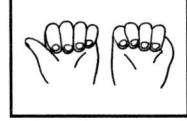

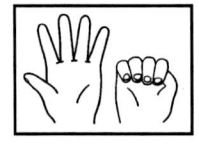

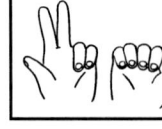

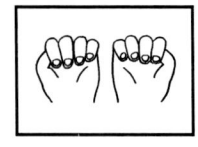

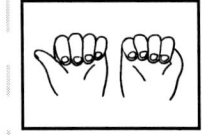

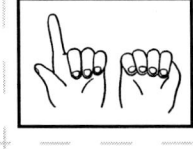

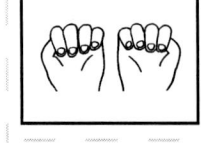

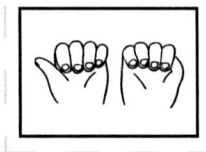

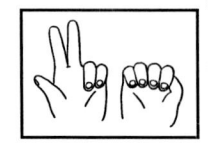

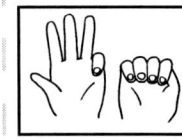

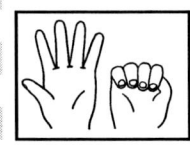

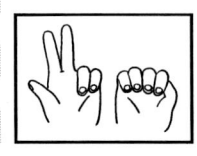

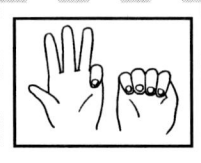

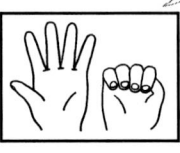

1 + ___ = 5

5 − 0 = ___

0 + ___ = 5

5 − 4 = ___

5 + ___ = 5

5 − 2 = ___

3 + ___ = 5

5 − 5 = ___

4 + ___ = 5

5 − 1 = ___

2 + ___ = 5

5 − 3 = ___

I am learning to make groupings within 5.

Colour the jigsaw pieces that add to: 4 red, 3 green and 5 blue.

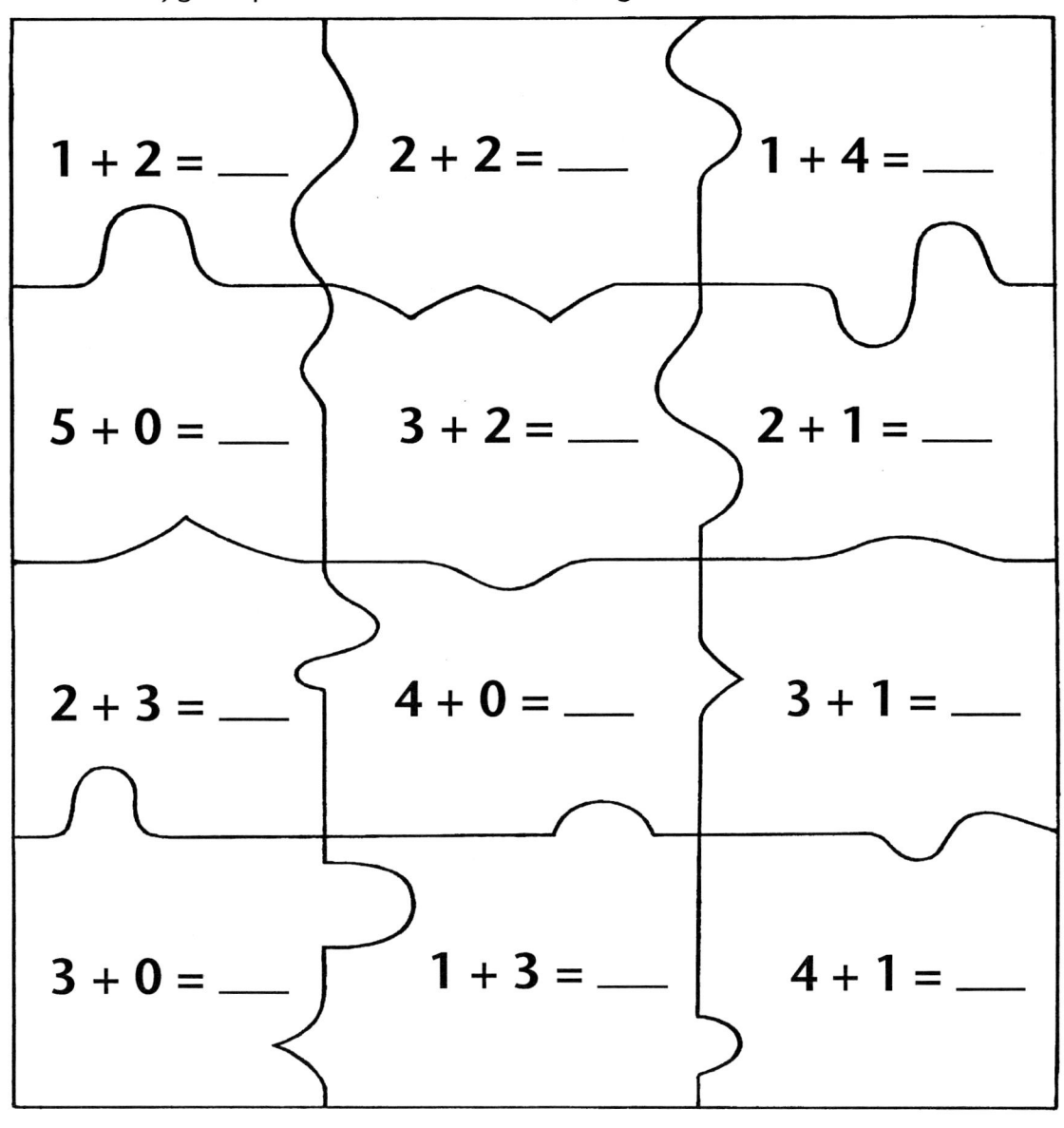

1 + 2 = ___	2 + 2 = ___	1 + 4 = ___
5 + 0 = ___	3 + 2 = ___	2 + 1 = ___
2 + 3 = ___	4 + 0 = ___	3 + 1 = ___
3 + 0 = ___	1 + 3 = ___	4 + 1 = ___

Complete the number sentences.

3 + 2 = ___	3 + 0 = ___	2 + 0 = ___
___ + 0 = 1	___ + 2 = 4	___ + 1 = 2
5 + ___ = 5	1 + ___ = 4	2 + ___ = 5
4 + 1 = ___	3 + 1 = ___	1 + 2 = ___
___ + 4 = 4	0 + ___ = 2	1 + ___ = 1
2 + 2 = ___	0 + ___ = 3	0 + ___ = 5

I am learning to make groupings within 10.

Colour the jigsaw pieces that add to 6 red, 7 green, 8 blue, 9 yellow and 10 orange.

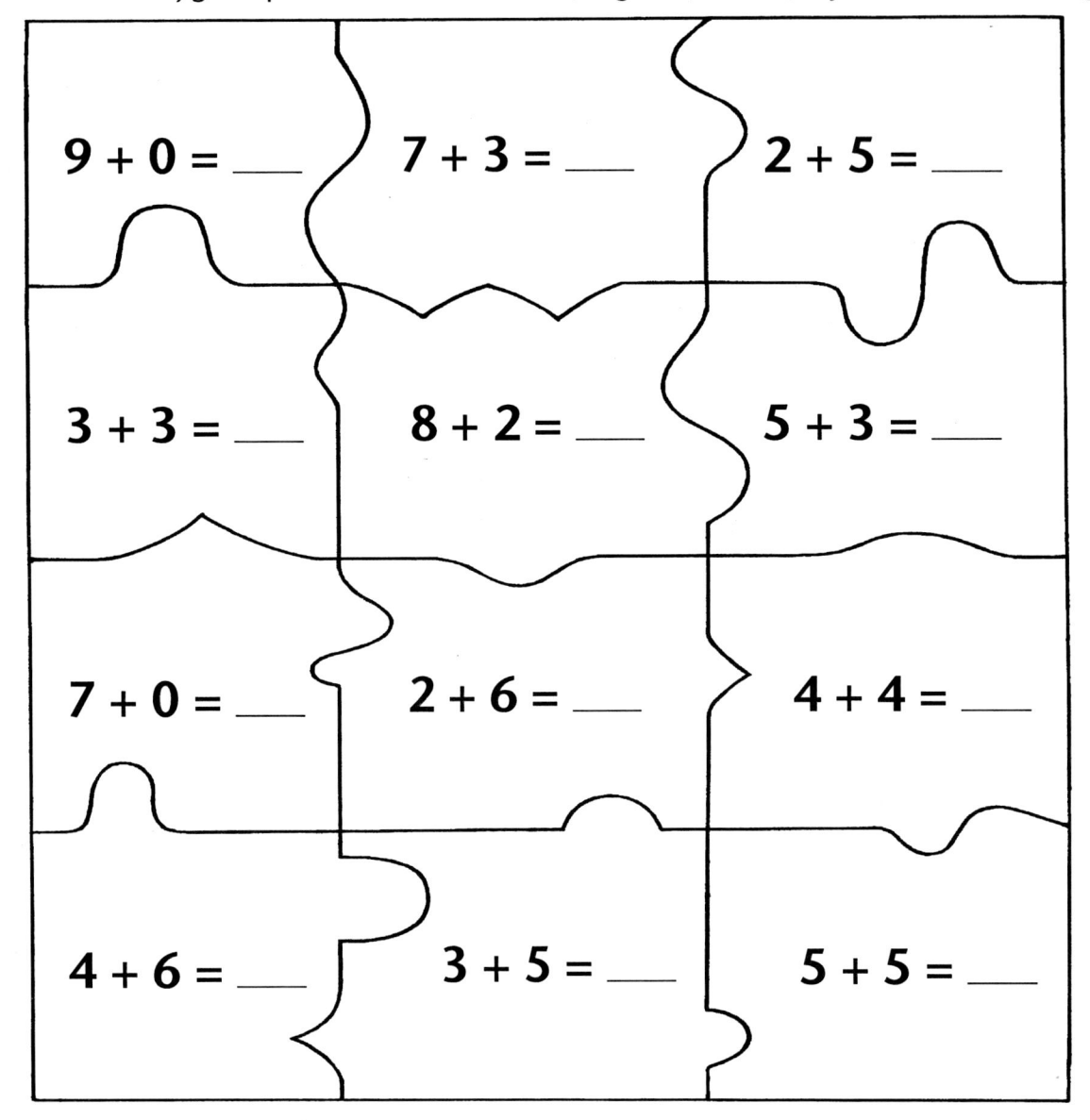

9 + 0 = ___	7 + 3 = ___	2 + 5 = ___
3 + 3 = ___	8 + 2 = ___	5 + 3 = ___
7 + 0 = ___	2 + 6 = ___	4 + 4 = ___
4 + 6 = ___	3 + 5 = ___	5 + 5 = ___

Complete the number sentences.

5 + 0 = ___	4 + 3 = ___	2 + 6 = ___
___ + 7 = 9	___ + 1 = 9	___ + 5 = 9
3 + ___ = 7	6 + ___ = 8	3 + ___ = 10
4 + 2 = ___	3 + 2 = ___	8 + 0 = ___
___ + 4 = 9	7 + ___ = 9	3 + ___ = 8
7 + 1 = ___	6 + ___ = 9	4 + ___ = 5

I am learning to make groupings within 10.

Colour the jigsaw pieces that add to: 6 red, 7 green, 8 blue, 9 yellow and 10 orange.

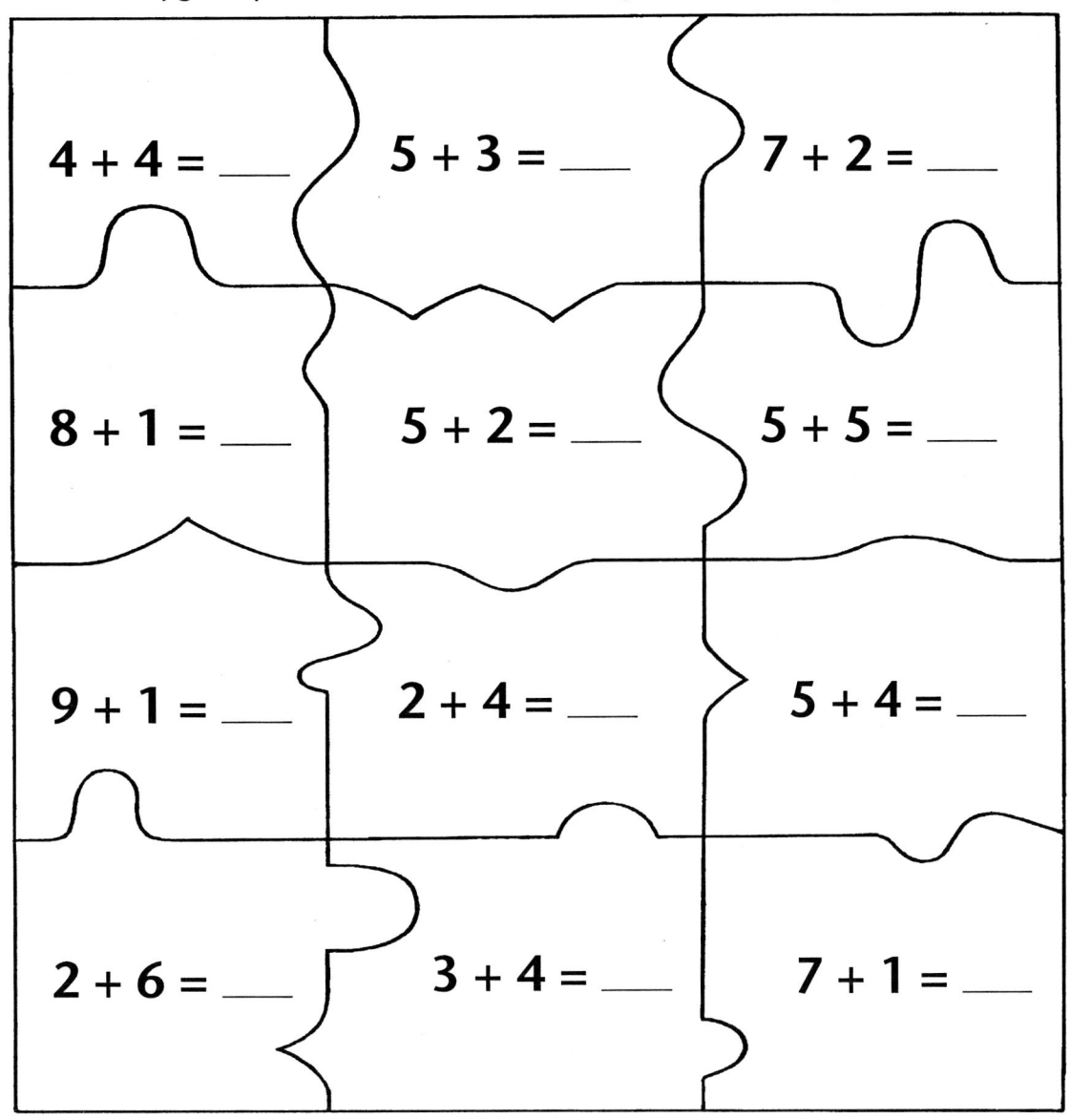

4 + 4 = ___	5 + 3 = ___	7 + 2 = ___
8 + 1 = ___	5 + 2 = ___	5 + 5 = ___
9 + 1 = ___	2 + 4 = ___	5 + 4 = ___
2 + 6 = ___	3 + 4 = ___	7 + 1 = ___

Complete the number sentences.

4 + 0 = ___	8 + 2 = ___	2 + 5 = ___
___ + 6 = 9	___ + 3 = 10	___ + 0 = 9
3 + ___ = 4	6 + ___ = 10	7 + ___ = 7
3 + 0 = ___	5 + 5 = ___	6 + 1 = ___
___ + 8 = 10	2 + ___ = 2	5 + ___ = 8
10 + 0 = ___	3 + ___ = 6	6 + ___ = 6

Solving addition problems by counting

I am learning to solve addition problems by counting all the objects.

Complete the number sentences by counting all the balls.

1 and 1 makes ____
1 + 1 = ____

2 and 1 makes ____
2 + 1 = ____

3 and 1 makes ____
3 + 1 = ____

4 and 1 makes ____
4 + 1 = ____

5 and 1 makes ____
5 + 1 = ____

6 and 1 makes ____
6 + 1 = ____

7 and 1 makes ____
7 + 1 = ____

8 and 1 makes ____
8 + 1 = ____

I am learning to solve addition problems by counting all the objects.

Complete the number sentences by counting all the balls.

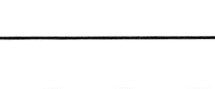

1 and 2 makes ____
1 + 2 = ____

2 and 2 makes ____
2 + 2 = ____

3 and 2 makes ____
3 + 2 = ____

4 and 2 makes ____
4 + 2 = ____

5 and 2 makes ____
5 + 2 = ____

6 and 2 makes ____
6 + 2 = ____

7 and 2 makes ____
7 + 2 = ____

8 and 2 makes ____
8 + 2 = ____

Adding and taking away 1

I am learning to add one more.

The monsters have measles. Draw one more spot on each monster, then fill in the gaps.

(monster with 4 spots)	Draw one more spot. How many now? ____ ____ and 1 more is ____
(monster with 7 spots)	Draw one more spot. How many now? ____ ____ and 1 more is ____
(monster with 1 spot)	Draw one more spot. How many now? ____ ____ and 1 more is ____
(monster with 5 spots)	Draw one more spot. How many now? ____ ____ and 1 more is ____
(monster with 6 spots)	Draw one more spot. How many now? ____ ____ and 1 more is ____

I am learning to add one more.

The monsters have measles. Draw one more spot on each monster, then fill in the gaps.

 (monster with 6 spots)	Draw one more spot. How many now? ____ ____ and 1 more is ____
 (monster with 2 spots)	Draw one more spot. How many now? ____ ____ and 1 more is ____
 (monster with 9 spots)	Draw one more spot. How many now? ____ ____ and 1 more is ____
 (monster with 7 spots)	Draw one more spot. How many now? ____ ____ and 1 more is ____
 (monster with 3 spots)	Draw one more spot. How many now? ____ ____ and 1 more is ____

I am learning to count to 10 and to make one less.

The monsters have been sneaking in and eating the monster munches. Draw the munches that each monster leaves and then fill in the gap.

How many munches? ____	Draw the munches with one less.
	How many munches now? ____

How many munches? ____	Draw the munches with one less.
	How many munches now? ____

How many munches? ____	Draw the munches with one less.
	How many munches now? ____

Count the number of dots in each tens frame. Cross one out. How many dots now?

7 and one less is ____

7 – ____ = ____

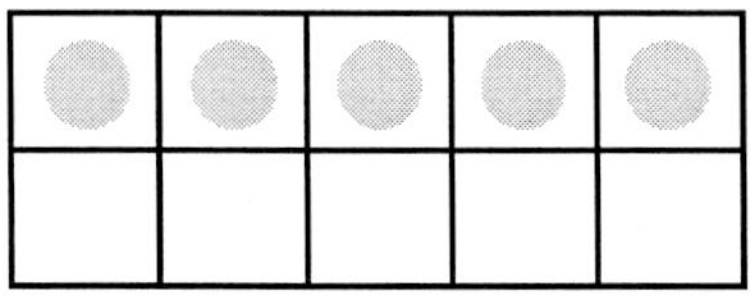

5 and one less is ____

5 – ____ = ____

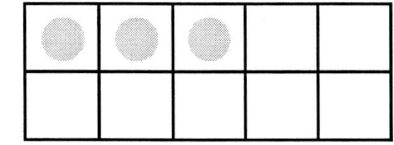

3 and one less is ____

3 – ____ = ____

I am learning to count to 10 and to make one less.

The monsters have been sneaking in and eating the monster munches. Draw the munches that each monster leaves and then fill in the gap.

How many munches? ____	Draw the munches with one less.
	How many munches now? ____

How many munches? ____	Draw the munches with one less.
	How many munches now? ____

How many munches? ____	Draw the munches with one less.
	How many munches now? ____

Count the number of dots in each tens frame. Cross one out. How many dots now?

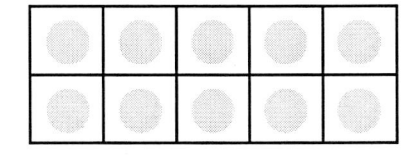

10 and one less is ____

10 – ____ = ____

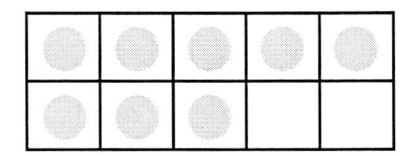

8 and one less is ____

8 – ____ = ____

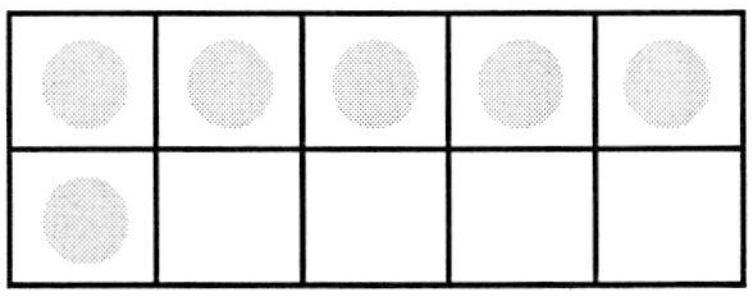

6 and one less is ____

6 – ____ = ____

I am learning to take away 1.

The monsters have measles. Cross out one spot on each monster, then fill in the gaps.

Cross out one spot.

How many now? ____

____ take away 1 is ____

____ – ____ = ____

Cross out one spot.

How many now? ____

____ take away 1 is ____

____ – ____ = ____

Cross out one spot.

How many now? ____

____ take away 1 is ____

____ – ____ = ____

Cross out one spot.

How many now? ____

____ take away 1 is ____

____ – ____ = ____

Cross out one spot.

How many now? ____

____ take away 1 is ____

____ – ____ = ____

I am learning to take away 1.

The monsters have measles. Cross out one spot on each monster, then fill in the gaps.

Cross out one spot.

How many now? ____

____ take away 1 is ____

____ − ____ = ____

Cross out one spot.

How many now? ____

____ take away 1 is ____

____ − ____ = ____

Cross out one spot.

How many now? ____

____ take away 1 is ____

____ − ____ = ____

Cross out one spot.

How many now? ____

____ take away 1 is ____

____ − ____ = ____

Cross out one spot.

How many now? ____

____ take away 1 is ____

____ − ____ = ____

Solving subtraction problems by counting

I am learning to solve subtraction problems by counting all the objects.

Solve each problem and write the number sentence.

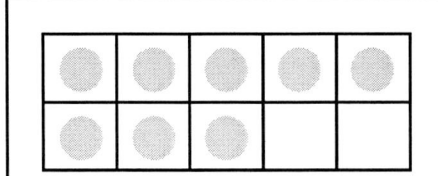

8 take away 2 makes ___ ___ − ___ = ___	9 take away 1 makes ___ ___ − ___ = ___
8 take away 4 makes ___ ___ − ___ = ___	6 take away 5 makes ___ ___ − ___ = ___
10 take away 2 makes ___ ___ − ___ = ___	7 take away 4 makes ___ ___ − ___ = ___
9 take away 6 makes ___ ___ − ___ = ___	6 take away 3 makes ___ ___ − ___ = ___

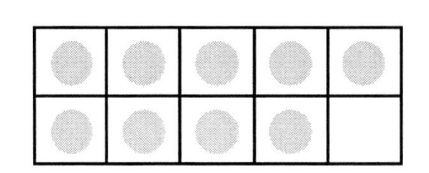

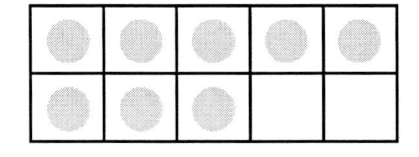

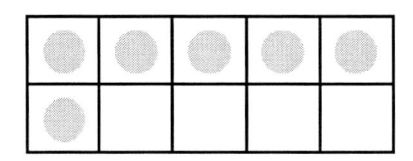

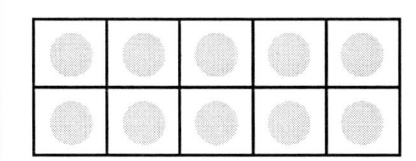

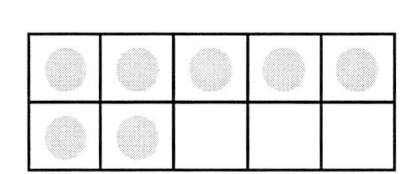

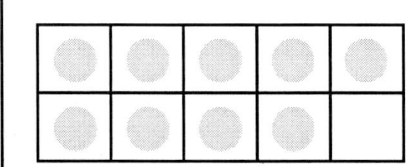

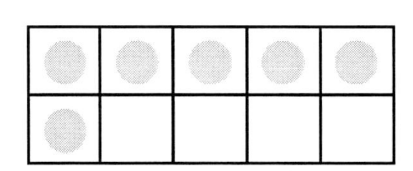

Complete the number sentences. Use the rugby balls on the right if you need to.

6 − 4 = ___	___ − 2 = 4	4 − ___ = 2
2 − ___ = 1	9 − ___ = 5	___ − 3 = 6
___ − 0 = 2	5 − 2 = ___	9 − ___ = 3
7 − 3 = ___	8 − ___ = 2	6 − 3 = ___

I am learning to solve subtraction problems by counting all the objects.

Solve each problem and write the number sentence.

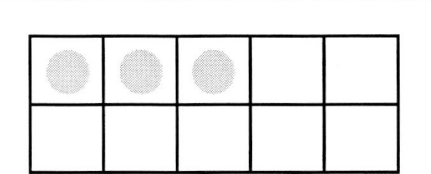

3 take away 2 makes ___
___ − ___ = ___

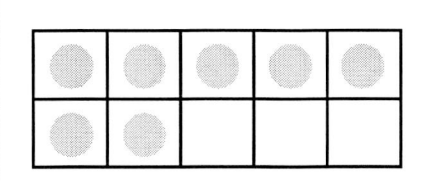

7 take away 6 makes ___
___ − ___ = ___

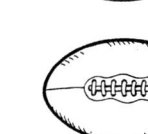

5 take away 3 makes ___
___ − ___ = ___

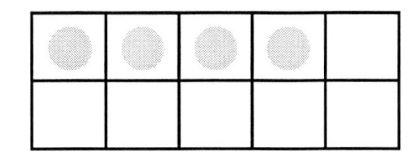

4 take away 2 makes ___
___ − ___ = ___

9 take away 5 makes ___
___ − ___ = ___

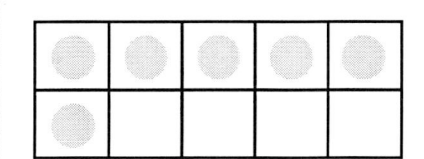

6 take away 4 makes ___
___ − ___ = ___

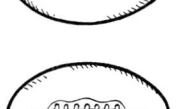

7 take away 2 makes ___
___ − ___ = ___

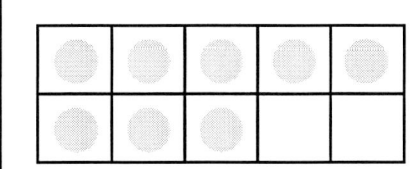

8 take away 3 makes ___
___ − ___ = ___

Complete the number sentences. Use the rugby balls on the right if you need to.

7 − 5 = ___   ___ − 2 = 3   3 − ___ = 2

2 − ___ = 0   8 − ___ = 5   ___ − 3 = 1

___ − 0 = 1   6 − 2 = ___   9 − ___ = 5

6 − 3 = ___   10 − ___ = 2   7 − 3 = ___

31

Recalling addition and subtraction facts

I am learning to instantly recall addition and subtraction facts to 5.

Colour each brick that = 5 red
= 4 blue
= 3 yellow
= 2 green
= 1 purple

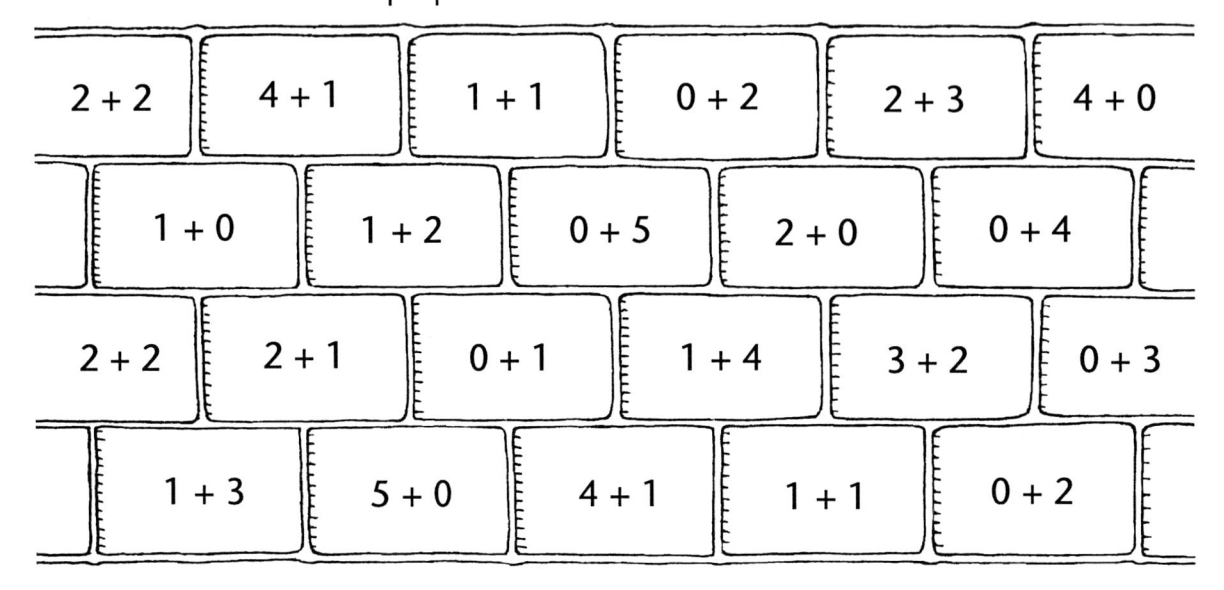

2 + 2	4 + 1	1 + 1	0 + 2	2 + 3	4 + 0
1 + 0	1 + 2	0 + 5	2 + 0	0 + 4
2 + 2	2 + 1	0 + 1	1 + 4	3 + 2	0 + 3
1 + 3	5 + 0	4 + 1	1 + 1	0 + 2

Colour in each brick that has a correct number sentence. If the number sentence is wrong, change it so that it is correct.

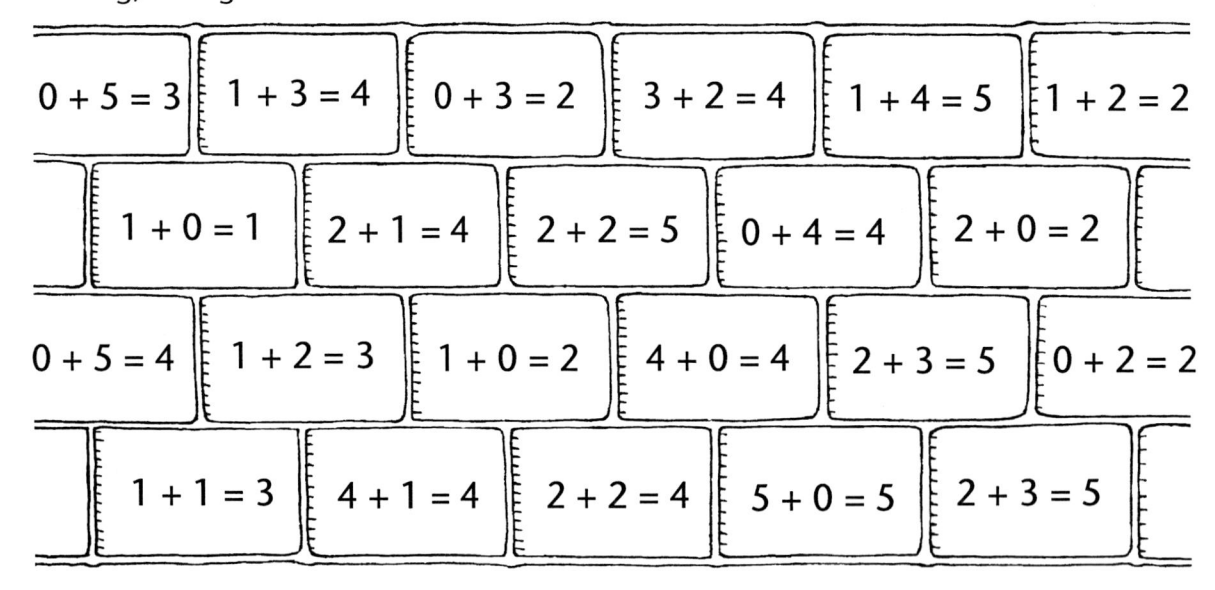

0 + 5 = 3	1 + 3 = 4	0 + 3 = 2	3 + 2 = 4	1 + 4 = 5	1 + 2 = 2
1 + 0 = 1	2 + 1 = 4	2 + 2 = 5	0 + 4 = 4	2 + 0 = 2
0 + 5 = 4	1 + 2 = 3	1 + 0 = 2	4 + 0 = 4	2 + 3 = 5	0 + 2 = 2
1 + 1 = 3	4 + 1 = 4	2 + 2 = 4	5 + 0 = 5	2 + 3 = 5

Complete the number sentences.

5 − 0 = ___   5 − 4 = ___   2 − 2 = ___

___ − 2 = 2   ___ − 3 = 0   ___ − 3 = 1

2 − ___ = 0   4 − ___ = 3   5 − ___ = 2

5 − 1 = ___   5 − 2 = ___   3 − 0 = ___

I am learning to instantly recall addition and subtraction facts to 10.

Colour each brick that = 10 red   5 = orange
                    = 9 blue   4 = brown
                    = 8 yellow   3 = pink
                    = 7 green   2 = grey
                    = 6 purple   1 = white

2 + 8	4 + 3	5 + 1	7 + 2	5 + 3	9 + 1
8 + 2	6 + 4	0 + 7	4 + 6	2 + 5
4 + 4	2 + 6	4 + 2	3 + 5	5 + 5	4 + 5
3 + 6	7 + 3	2 + 4	6 + 1	4 + 2

Colour in each brick that has a correct number sentence. If the number sentence is wrong, change it so that it is correct.

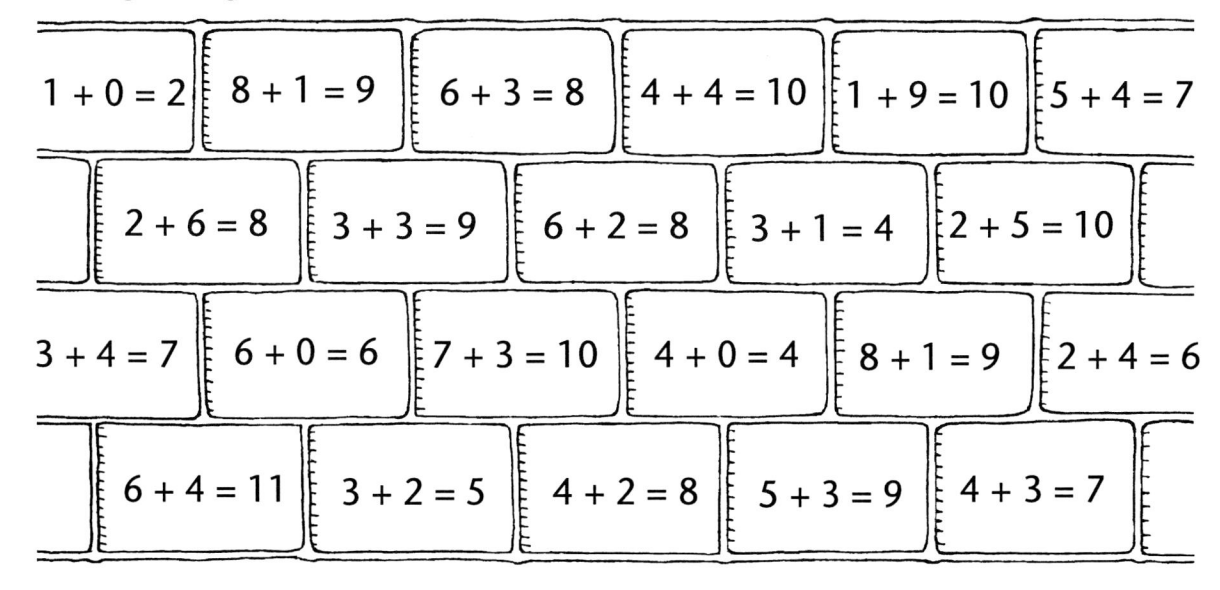

1 + 0 = 2	8 + 1 = 9	6 + 3 = 8	4 + 4 = 10	1 + 9 = 10	5 + 4 = 7
2 + 6 = 8	3 + 3 = 9	6 + 2 = 8	3 + 1 = 4	2 + 5 = 10
3 + 4 = 7	6 + 0 = 6	7 + 3 = 10	4 + 0 = 4	8 + 1 = 9	2 + 4 = 6
6 + 4 = 11	3 + 2 = 5	4 + 2 = 8	5 + 3 = 9	4 + 3 = 7

Complete the number sentences.

3 − 2 = ____   2 − 1 = ____   4 − 3 = ____

____ − 0 = 4   ____ − 0 = 5   ____ − 3 = 2

5 − ____ = 4   4 − ____ = 2   2 − ____ = 0

4 − 4 = ____   3 − 1 = ____   3 − 3 = ____

Counting in twos and fives

I am learning to count in twos to 20.

Count in twos to help you fill in the missing numbers in the elephant footprints.

I am learning to count in twos to 20.

Count in twos to help you fill in the missing numbers in each row.

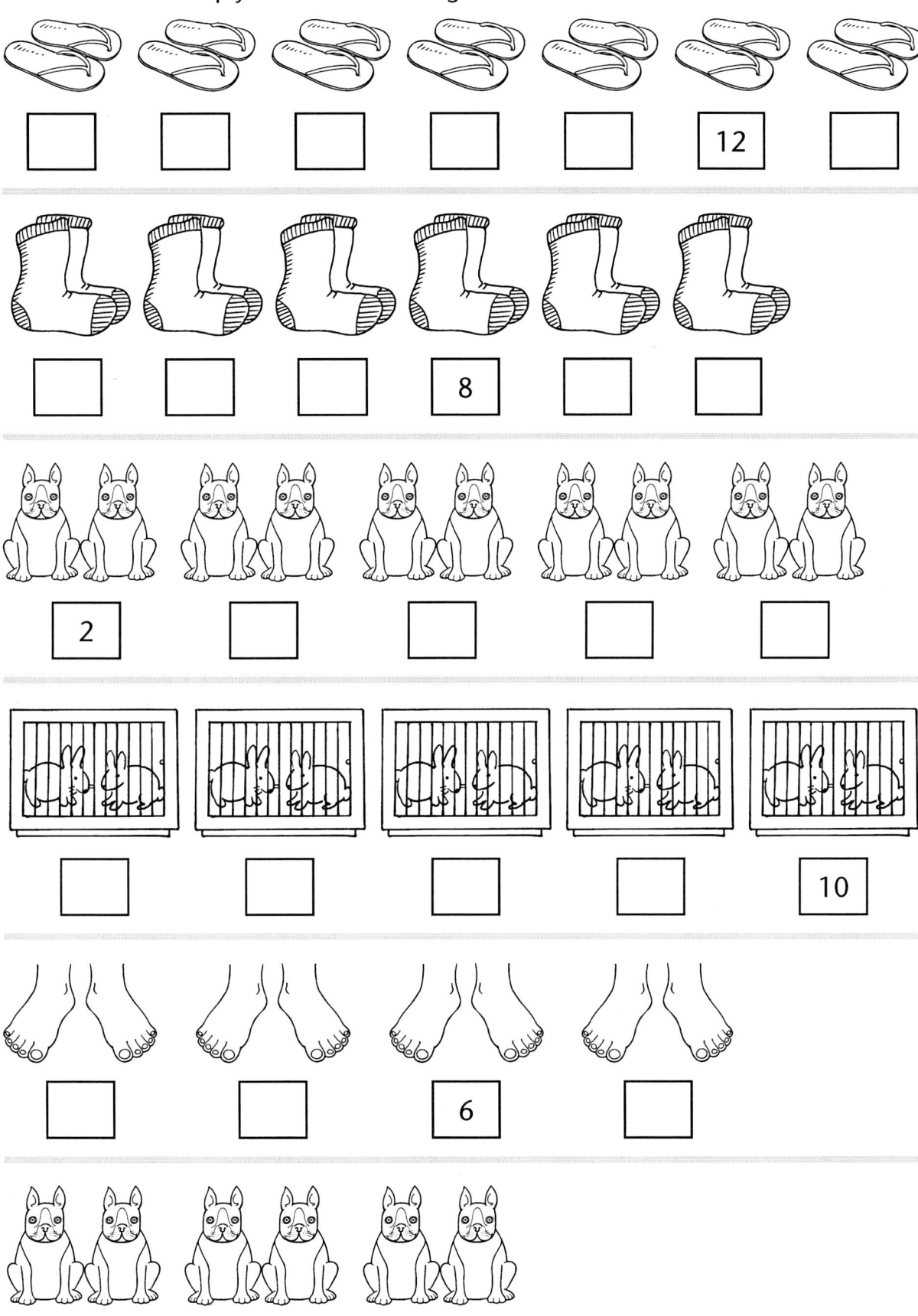

| 2 | 4 | 6 | 8 | 10 | 12 | 14 |

| 2 | 4 | 6 | 8 | 10 | 12 |

| 2 | 4 | 6 | 8 | 10 |

| 2 | 4 | 6 | 8 | 10 |

| 2 | 4 | 6 | 8 |

| 2 | 4 | 6 |

LI - understand the 5 times tables.

I am learning to count in fives to 20.

Count in fives to help you count the number of monster toes or fingers in each row.

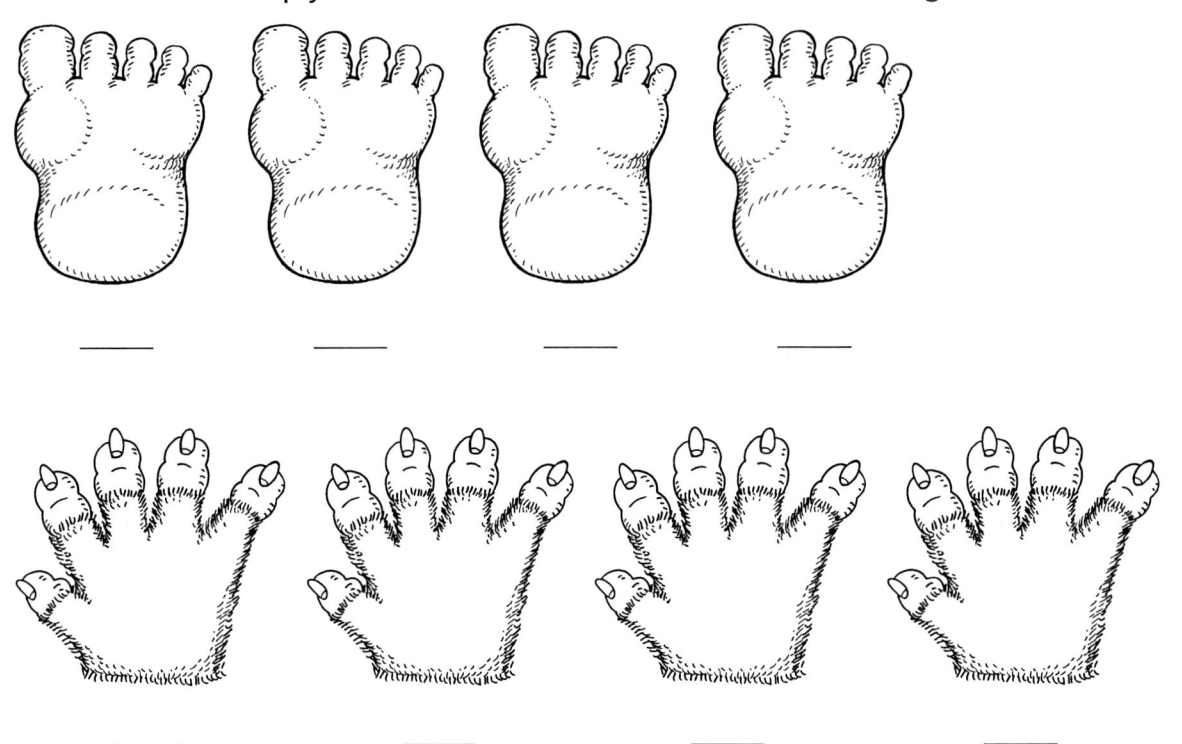

___ ___ ___ ___

___ ___ ___ ___

Count in fives to help you find a safe path through the monsters.

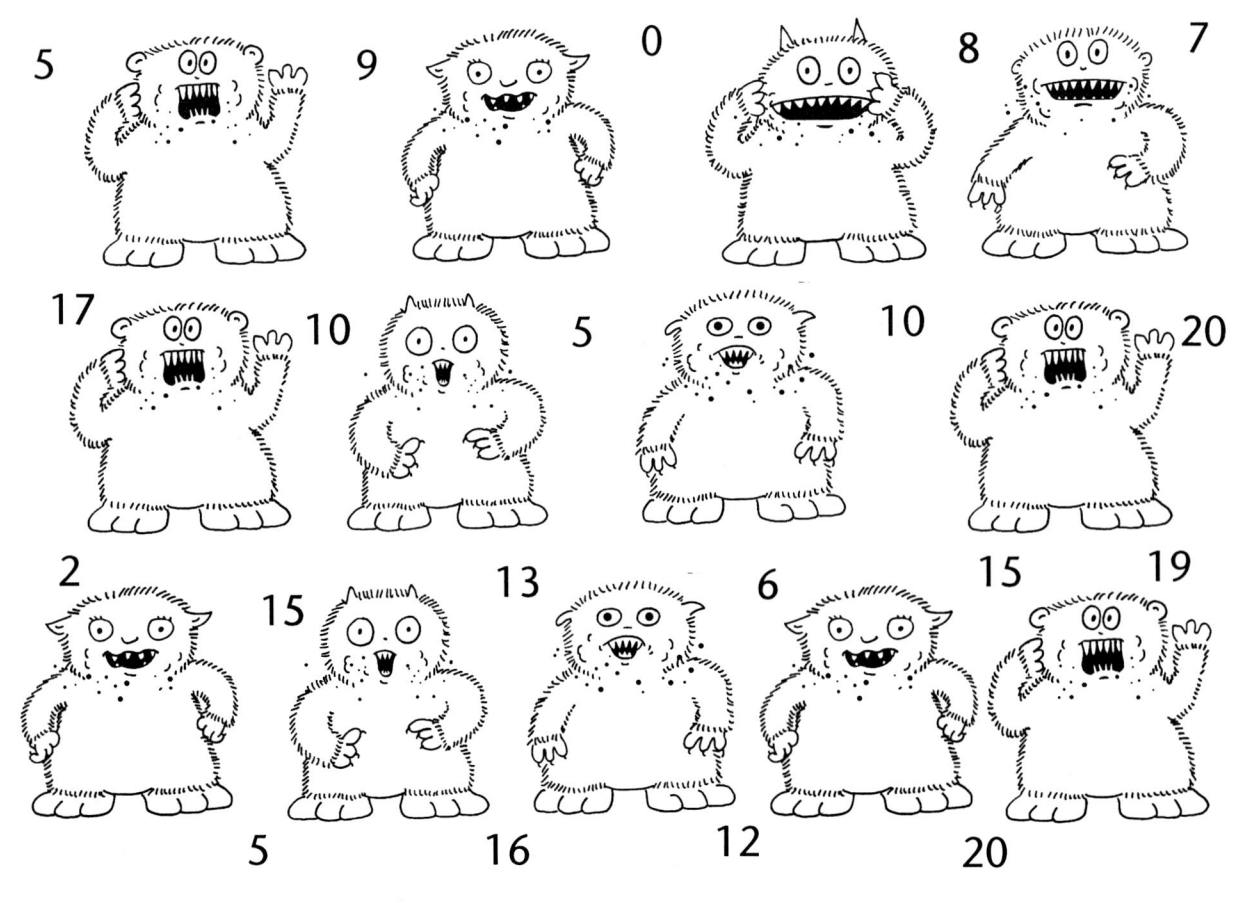

5   9   0   8   7

17   10   5   10   20

2   15   13   6   15   19

5   16   12   20

36

I am learning to count in fives to 20.

Count forwards and backwards in fives to help you fill in the missing numbers. The first one is done for you.

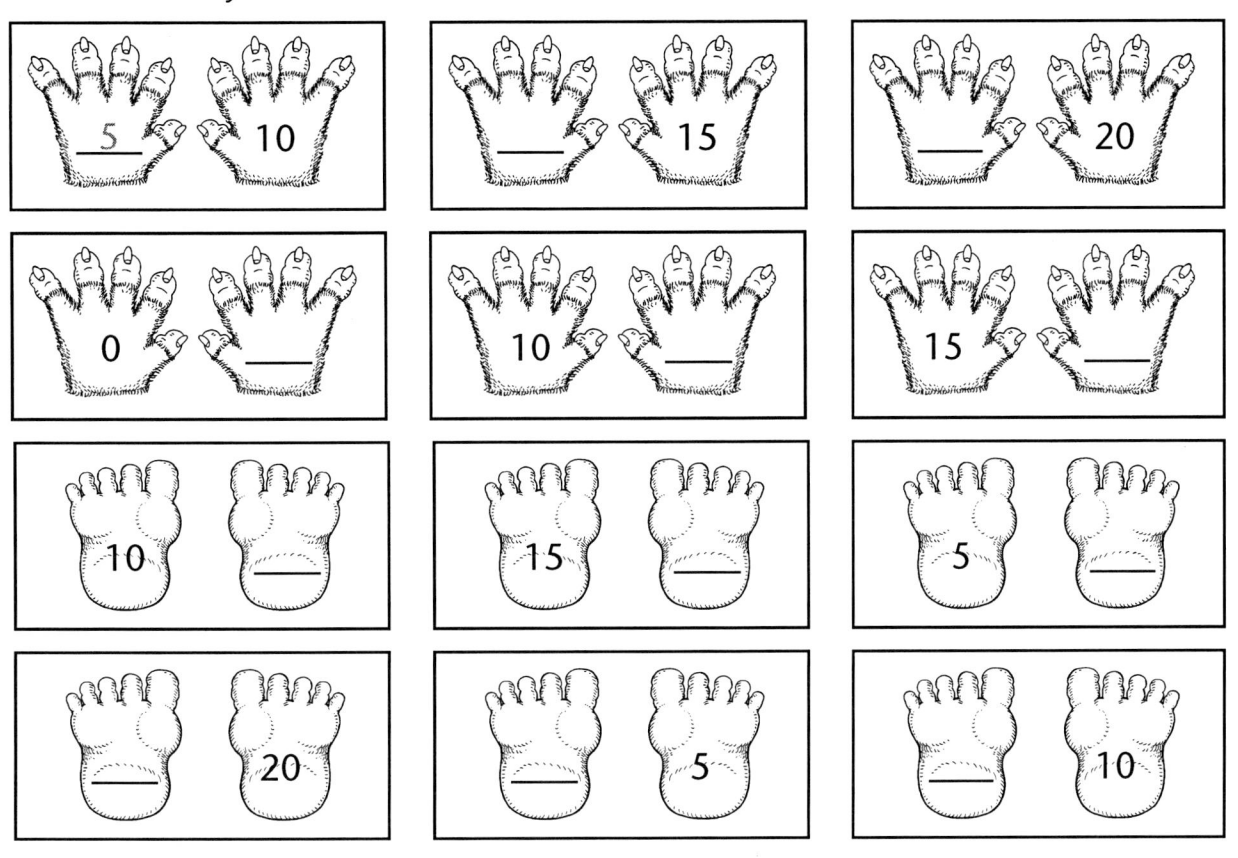

Count in fives to help you count the candles on each row of cakes.

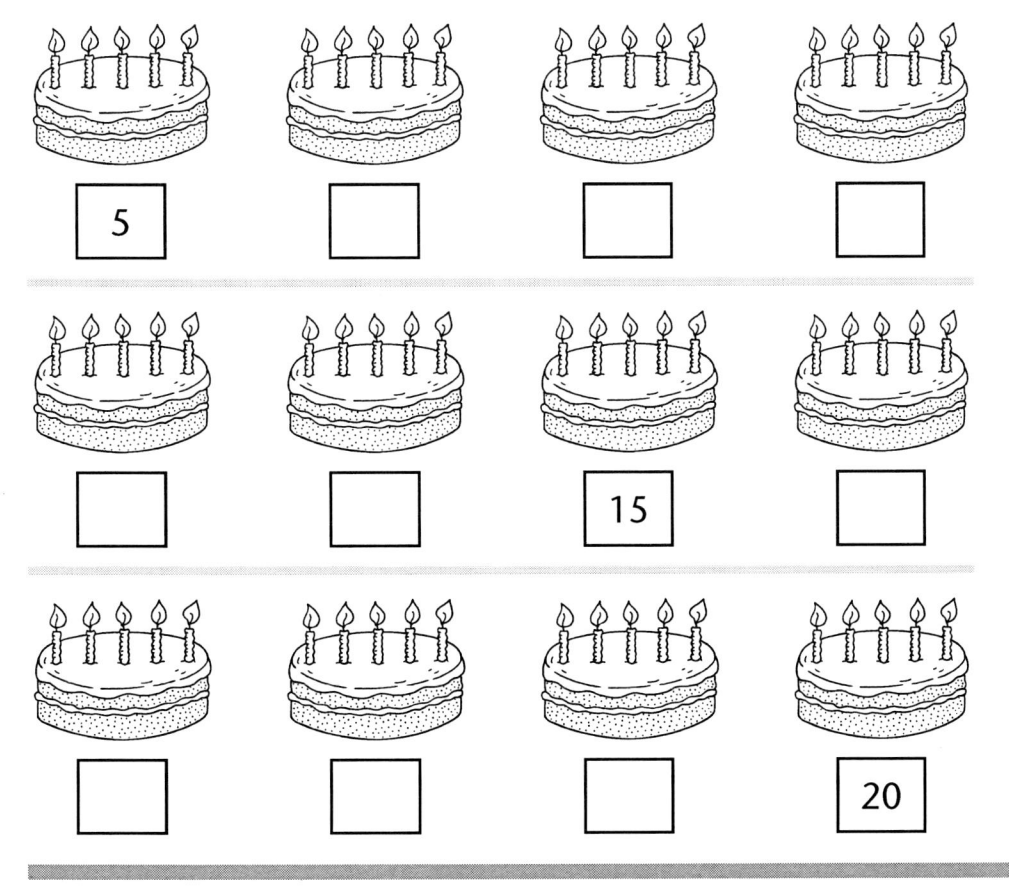

Showing and finding half

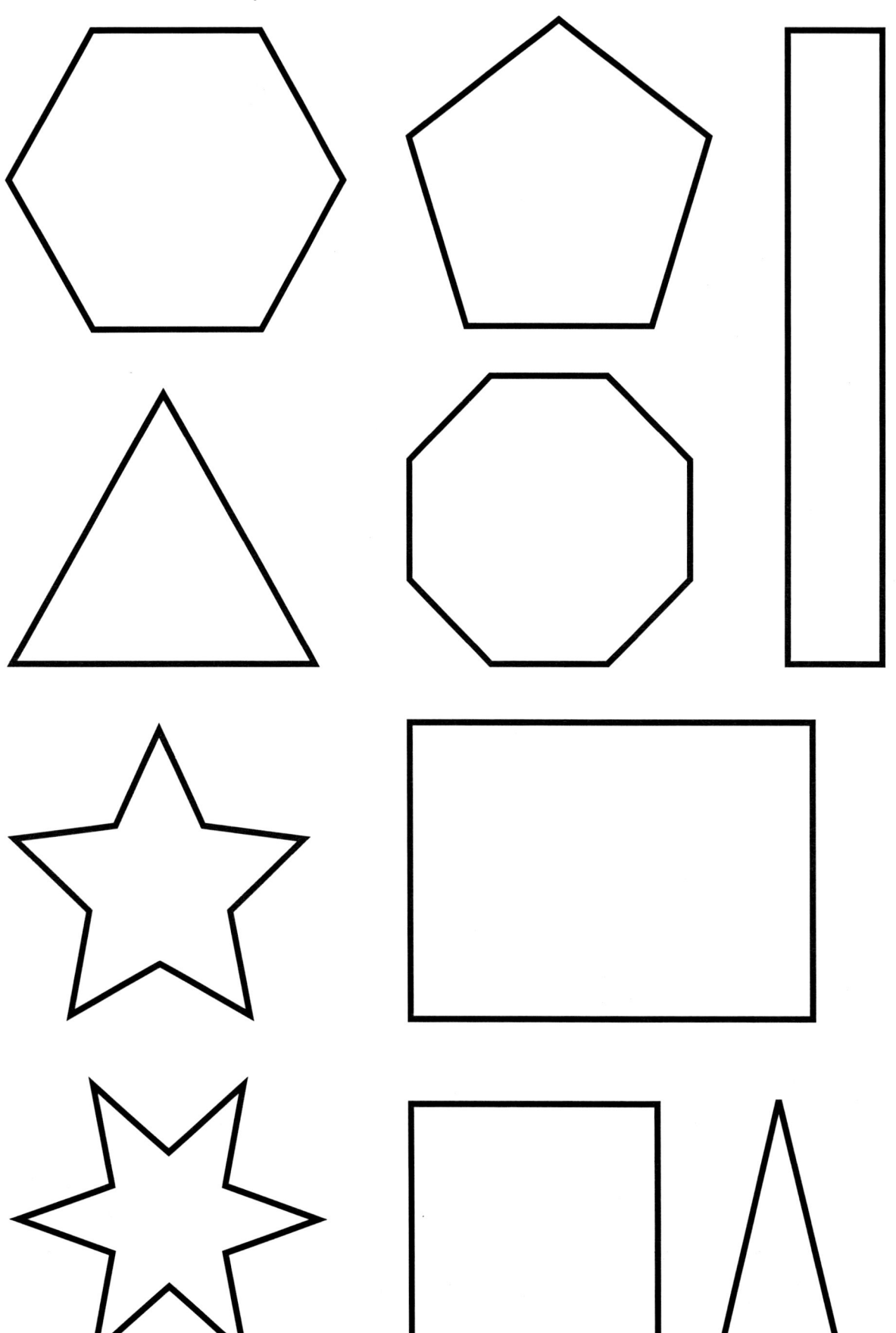

I am learning to show half of a shape.

Colour half of each shape.

I am learning to show half of a shape.

Colour half of each shape.

I am learning to find half of an object.

Draw the other half to finish the shape.

I am learning to find half of a set of objects to 20.

Colour half of each set of objects. Then finish the number sentence.

(4 skateboards)	Half of ___ is ___
(6 baskets)	Half of ___ is ___
(2 cars)	Half of ___ is ___
(10 candles)	Half of ___ is ___
(8 dogs)	Half of ___ is ___
(16 apples)	Half of ___ is ___
(14 sacks)	Half of ___ is ___
(12 mice)	Half of ___ is ___

41

I am learning to find half of a set of objects to 20.

Colour half of each set of objects. Then finish the number sentence.

(20 brushes)	Half of ____ is ____
(8 chocolate bars)	Half of ____ is ____
(16 mp3 players)	Half of ____ is ____
(16 basketballs)	Half of ____ is ____
(14 brushes)	Half of ____ is ____
(10 chocolate bars)	Half of ____ is ____
(12 mp3 players)	Half of ____ is ____
(6 basketballs)	Half of ____ is ____

42

Activity cards

Overview

Monster hands and feet
(pages 44–45)

To **make** the game:
- copy the cards onto coloured paper, laminate and cut up
- store the cards in a ziplock bag.

The cards can be **used** in a variety of ways:
- children can count in fives or twos and use a whiteboard marker to write the numerals on each card
- addition and subtraction number sentences can be written on each card and the children can fill in the answer.

Before and after (page 46)

To **make** the activity:
- copy the cards (including a set of number cards from page 51–52) onto coloured paper, laminate and cut up
- store the cards in a ziplock bag.

To **use**:
- place a set of number cards upside down
- in turn, children turn one number card over and place it on the blank rectangle in the centre of the game board
- using a whiteboard pen or another set of number cards, record as many numbers as you can that come before and after the number card that was turned over.

Before and after bingo (page 47)

To **make** the activity:
- copy the cards (including a set of number cards from page 51–52) onto coloured paper, laminate and cut up
- store the cards in a ziplock bag.

To **play**:
- give each child a game board
- place a pile of number cards in the centre
- in turn, each child turns over one number card – if any of the children has a number on their game board that comes directly before or after this number card, they cover it with a counter
- the first child to cover all of the numbers on their board is the winner.

Addition and subtraction carrots
(pages 48–49)

Aim: To reinforce addition and subtraction number facts.

To **make** the cards:
- copy the cards onto coloured paper
- write the appropriate numbers in the squares
- laminate the cards.

To **use** addition and subtraction carrots:
- the children work their way through the cards, filling in the missing numbers to complete the number sentences with a whiteboard pen.

Make it (pages 50–55)

Aim: To reinforce finger patterns to 5, 10 and 20.

To **prepare** the game:
- copy four sets of number cards onto coloured paper
- laminate the number cards, cut them up and store them in a ziplock bag
- copy the game boards (making 5, 10 or 20) – one for each player.

To **play** the game of number facts for five:
- spread all of the cards face down
- the first player turns over two cards – if they make a number fact for five, the player keeps the cards and puts them on their game board; if not the cards are returned and the next player has a turn
- the player who ends up with the most pairs is the winner.

The same procedure can be followed for Make it 10 and Make it 20.

Monster hands and feet

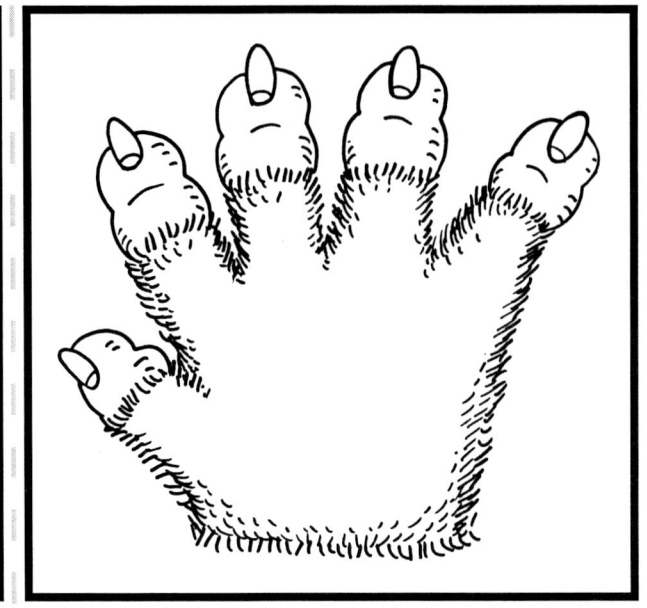

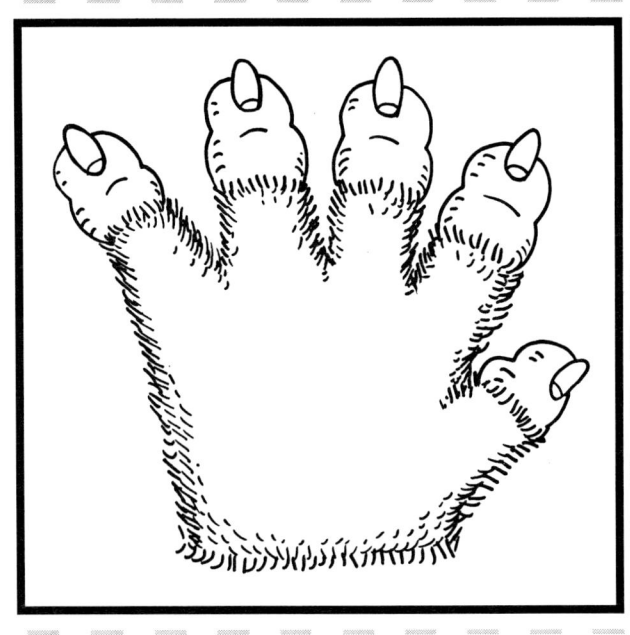

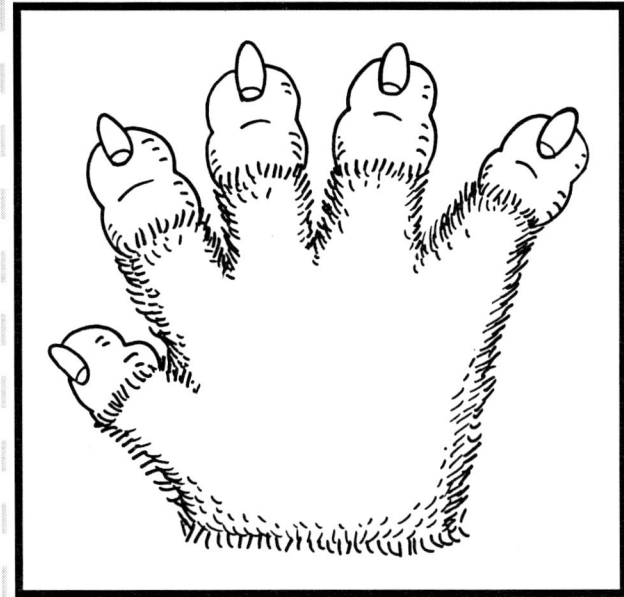

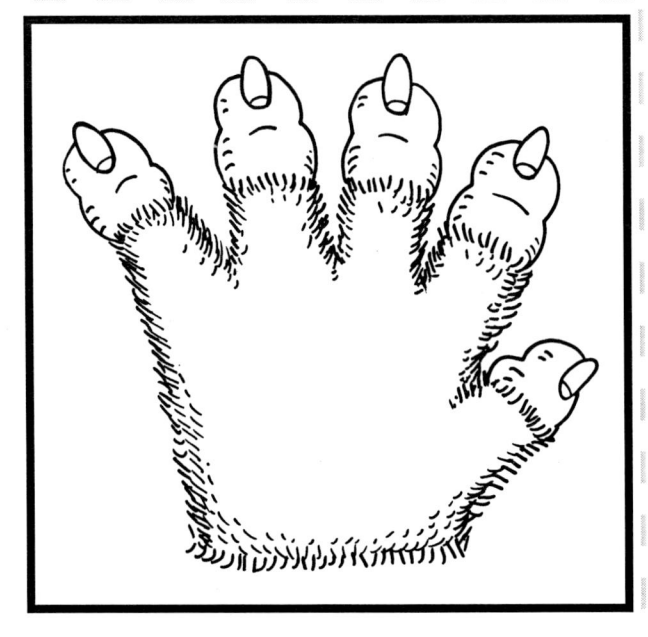

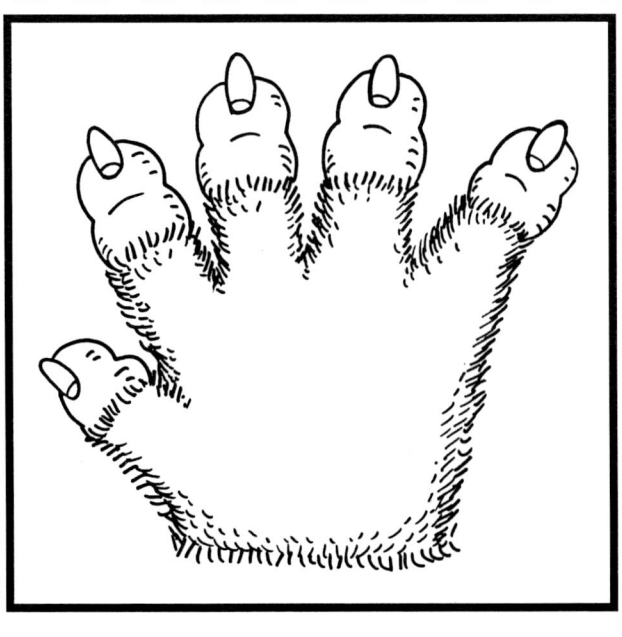

Monster hands and feet

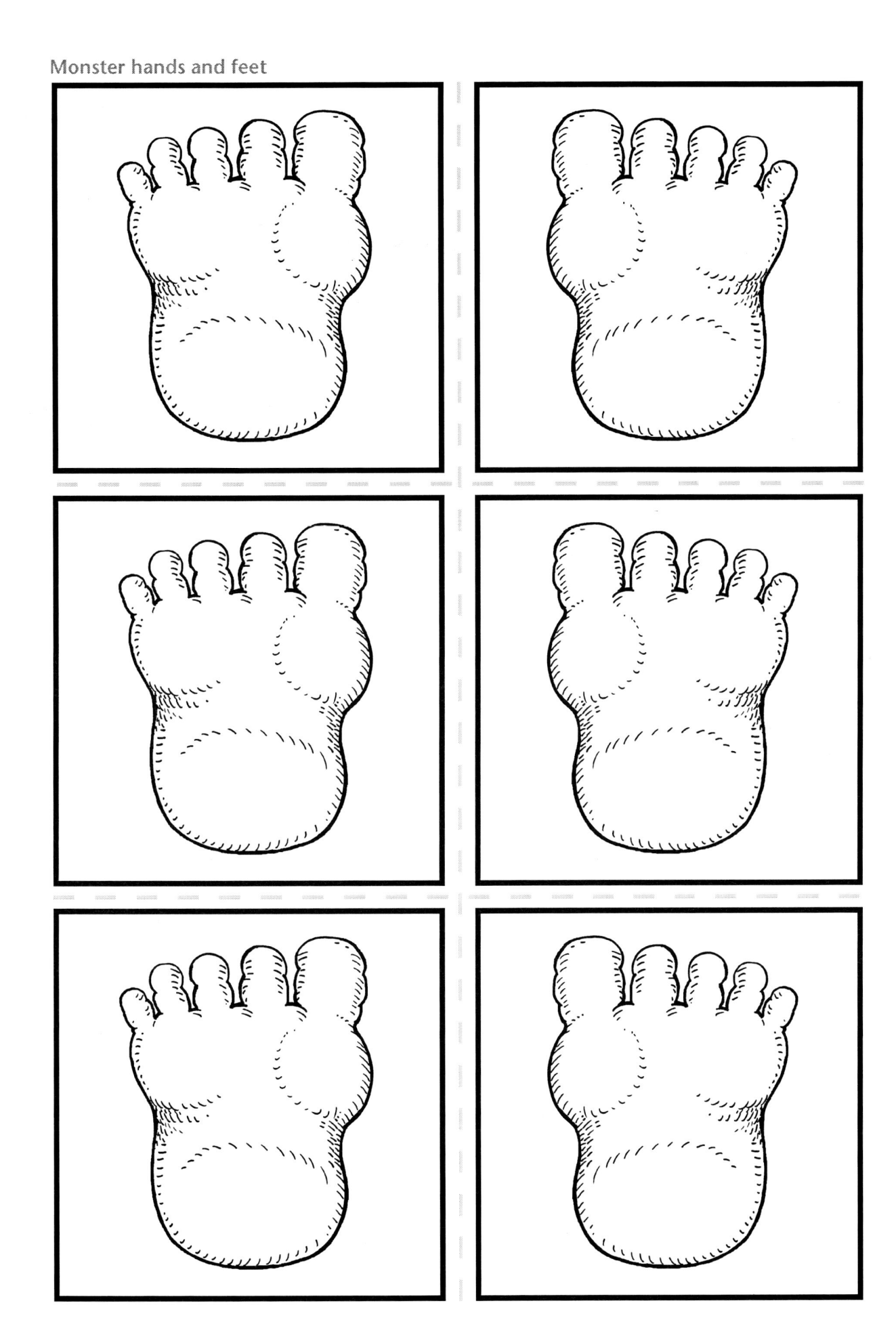

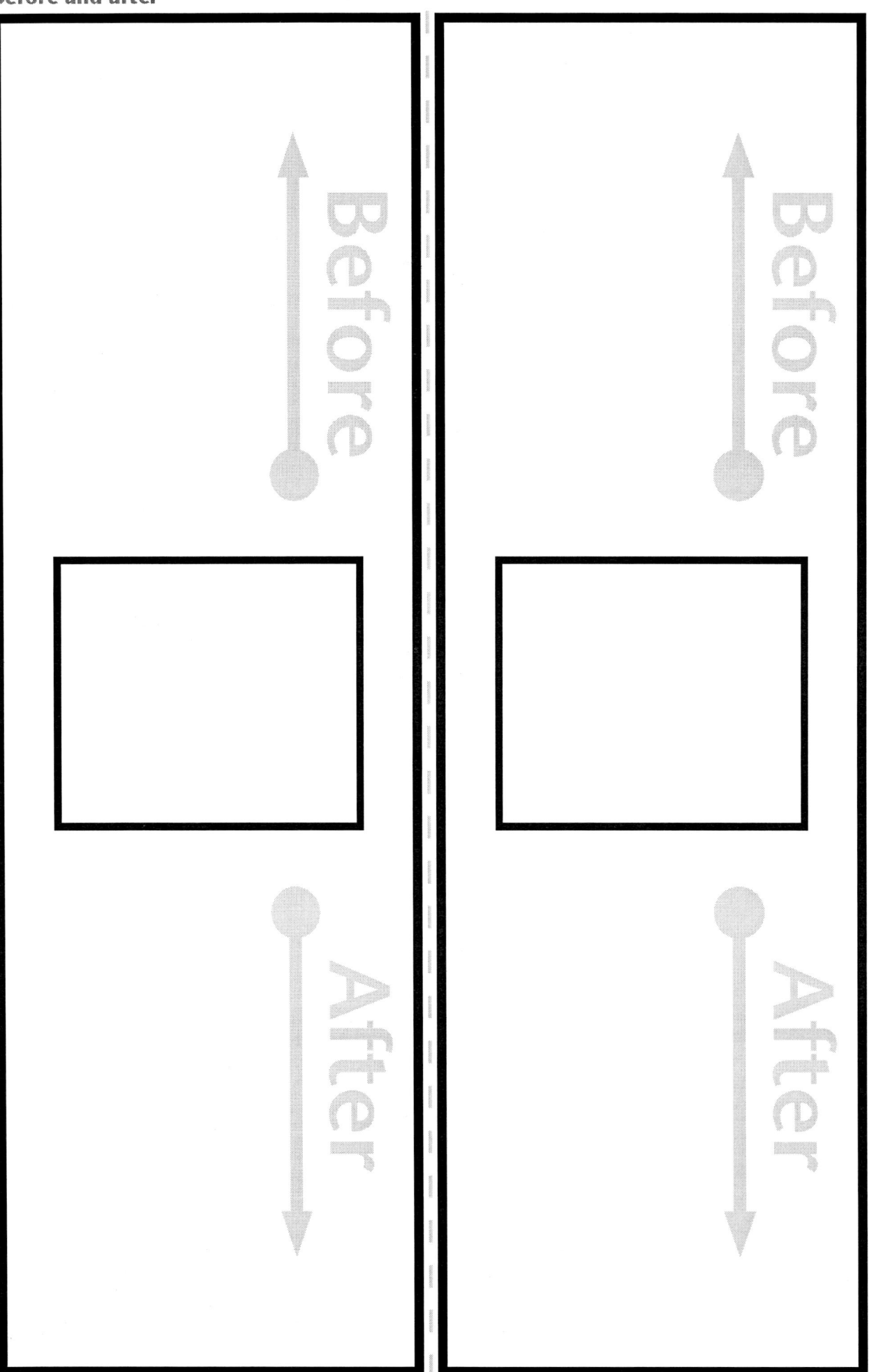

Before and after

Before and after bingo

6	11	14	9
16	2	7	17
8	10	15	12

5	10	13	8
15	3	6	16
7	9	11	4

7	12	5	10
17	4	8	18
9	11	16	13

Addition and subtraction carrots

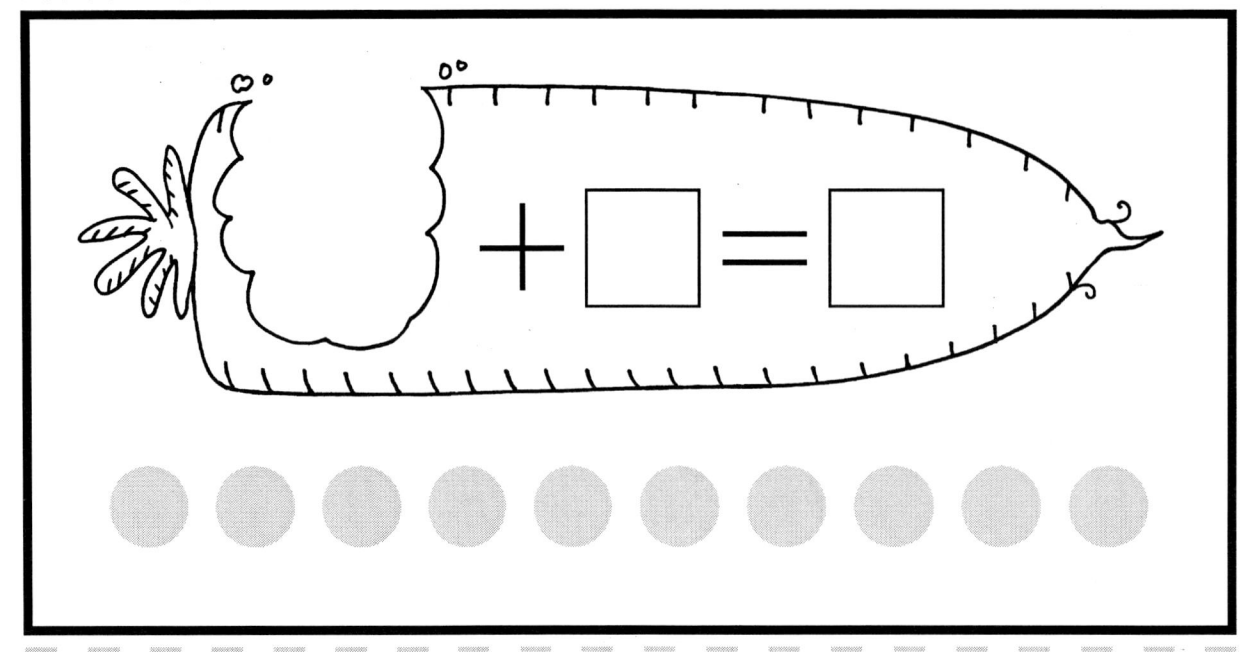

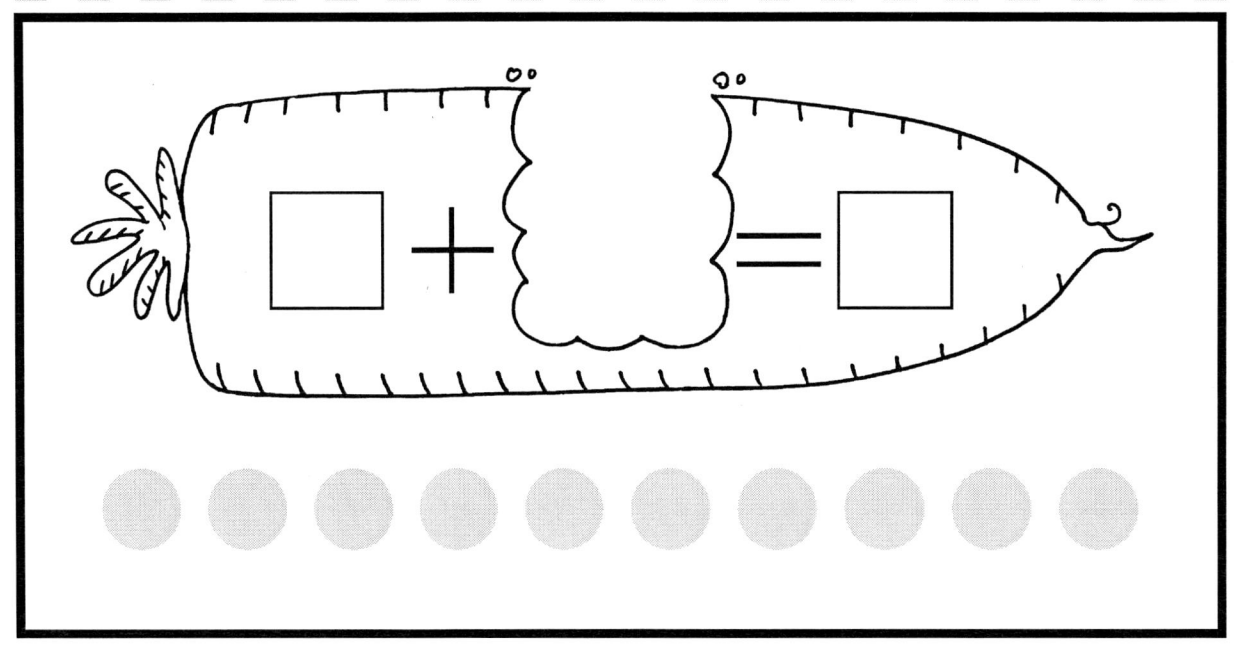

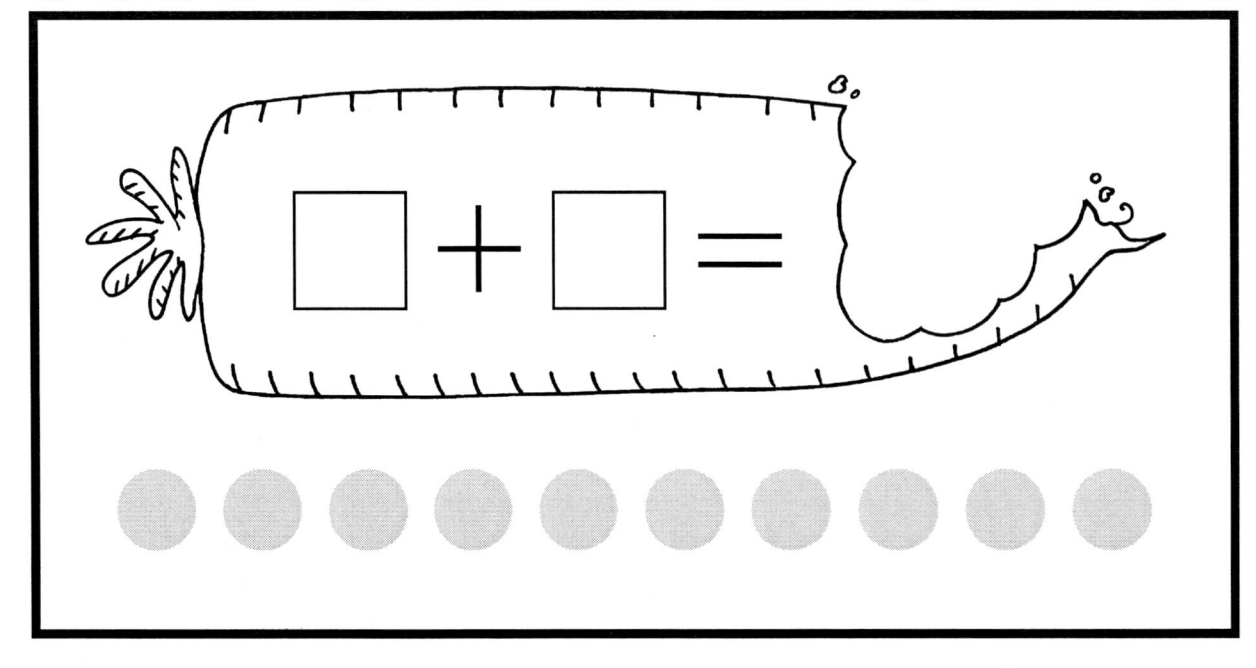

Addition and subtraction carrots

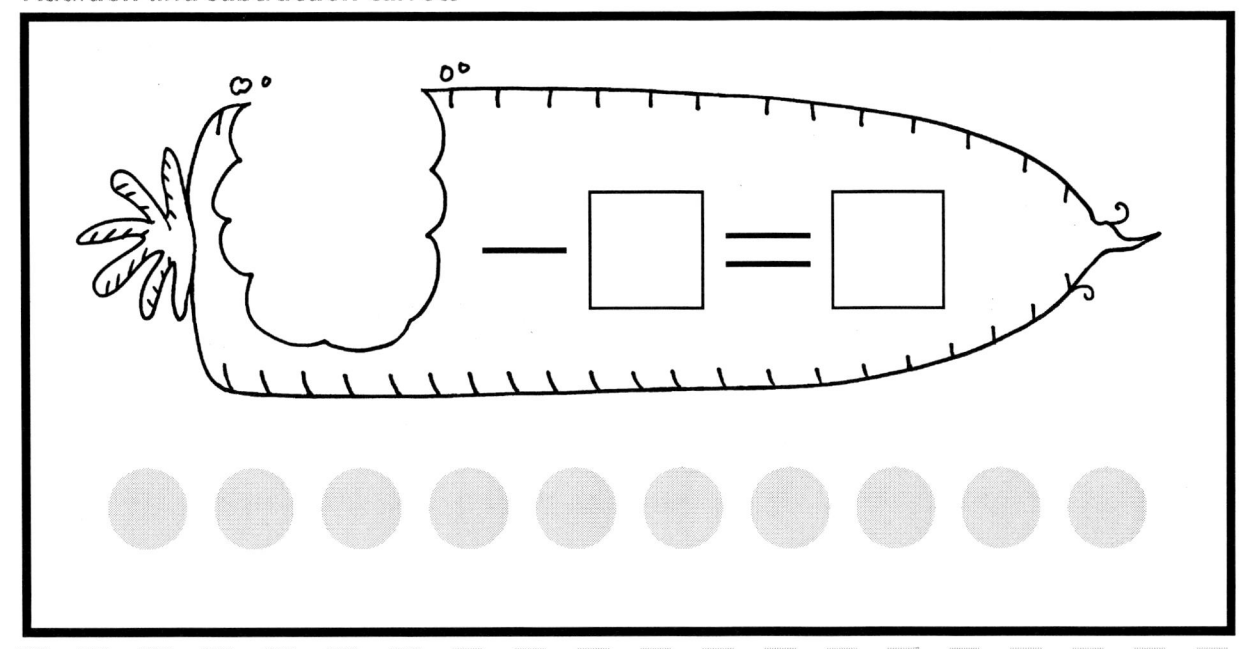

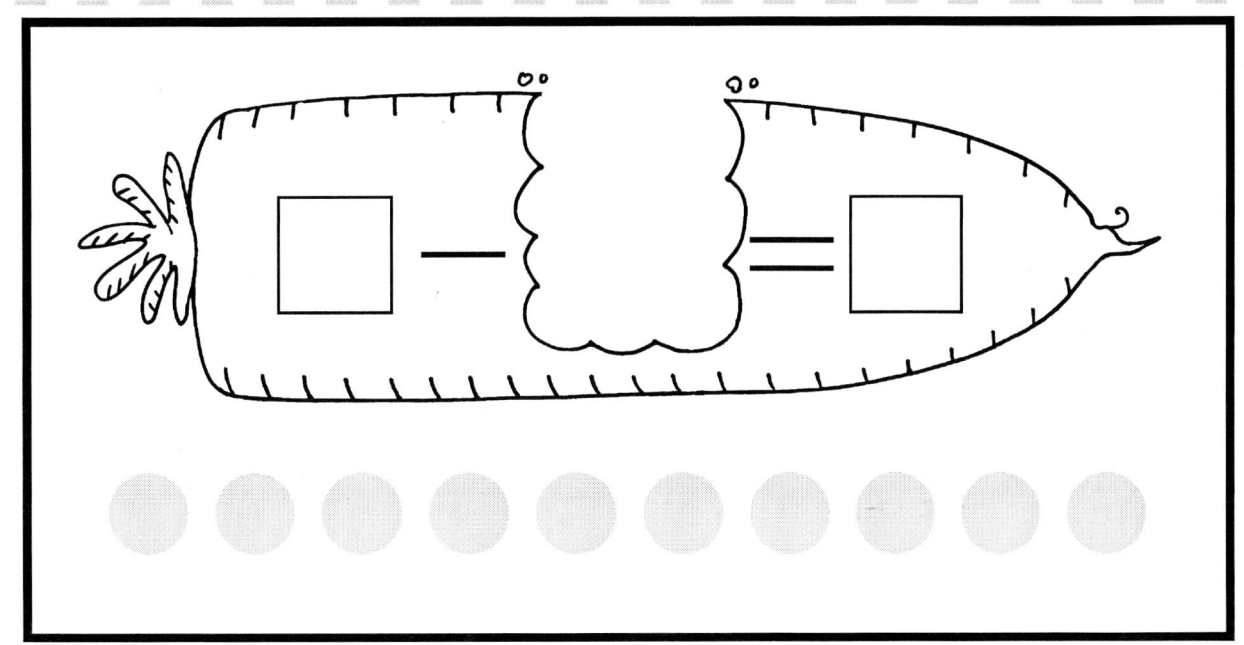

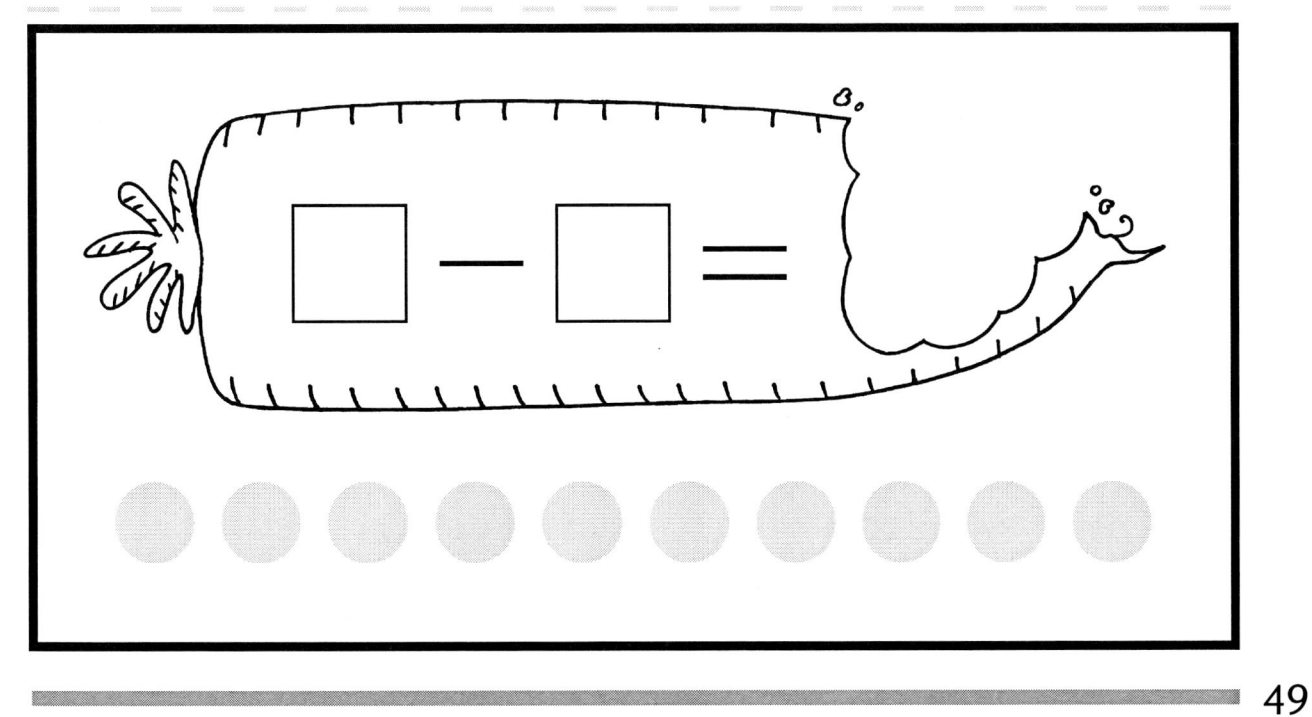

Make it (number cards)

0	1	2
3	4	5
0	1	2
3	4	5

Make it (number cards)

0	1	2
3	4	5
6	7	8
9	10	

Make it (number cards)

11	12	13
14	15	16
17	18	19
20		

Make it (game boards)

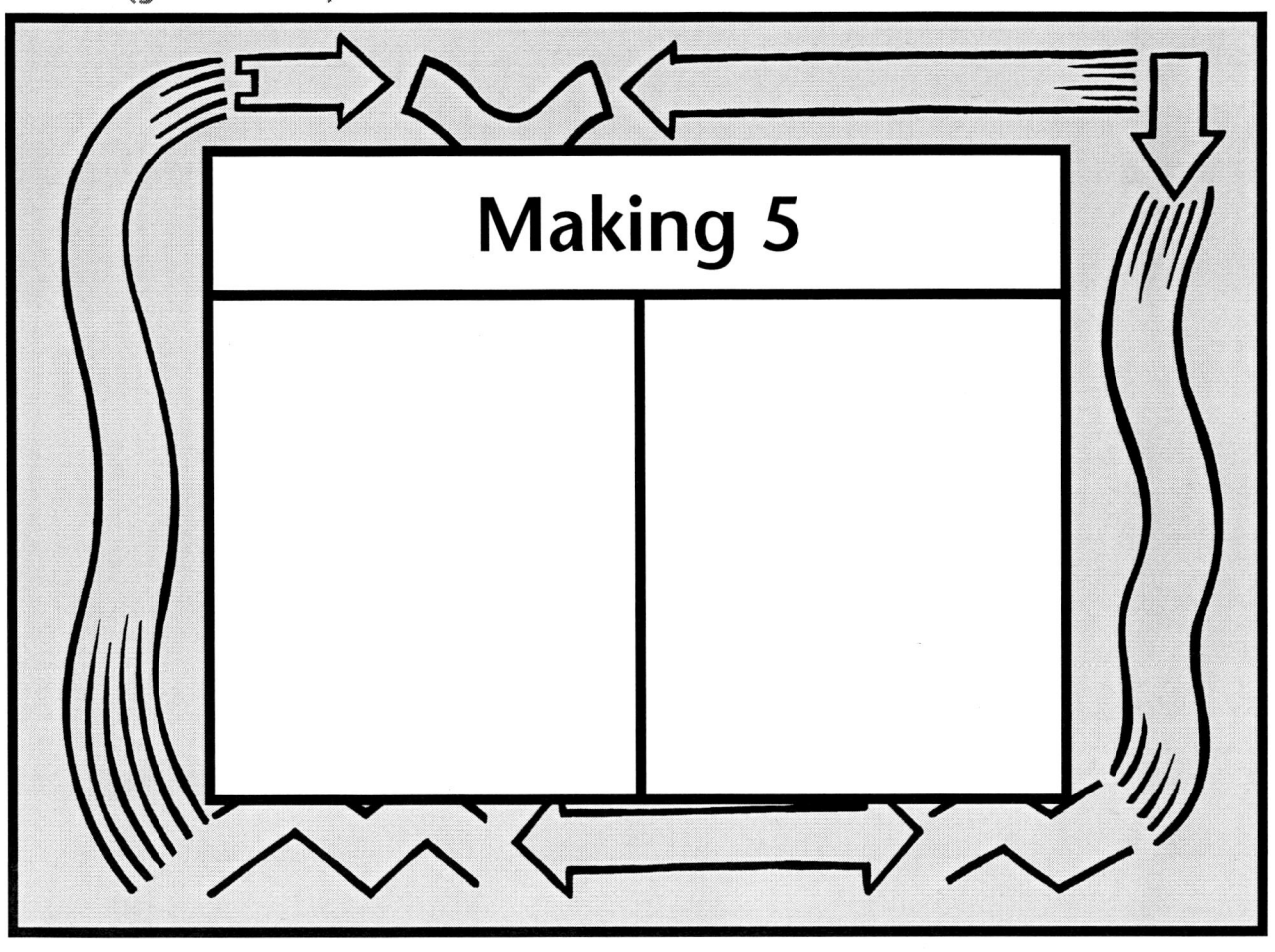

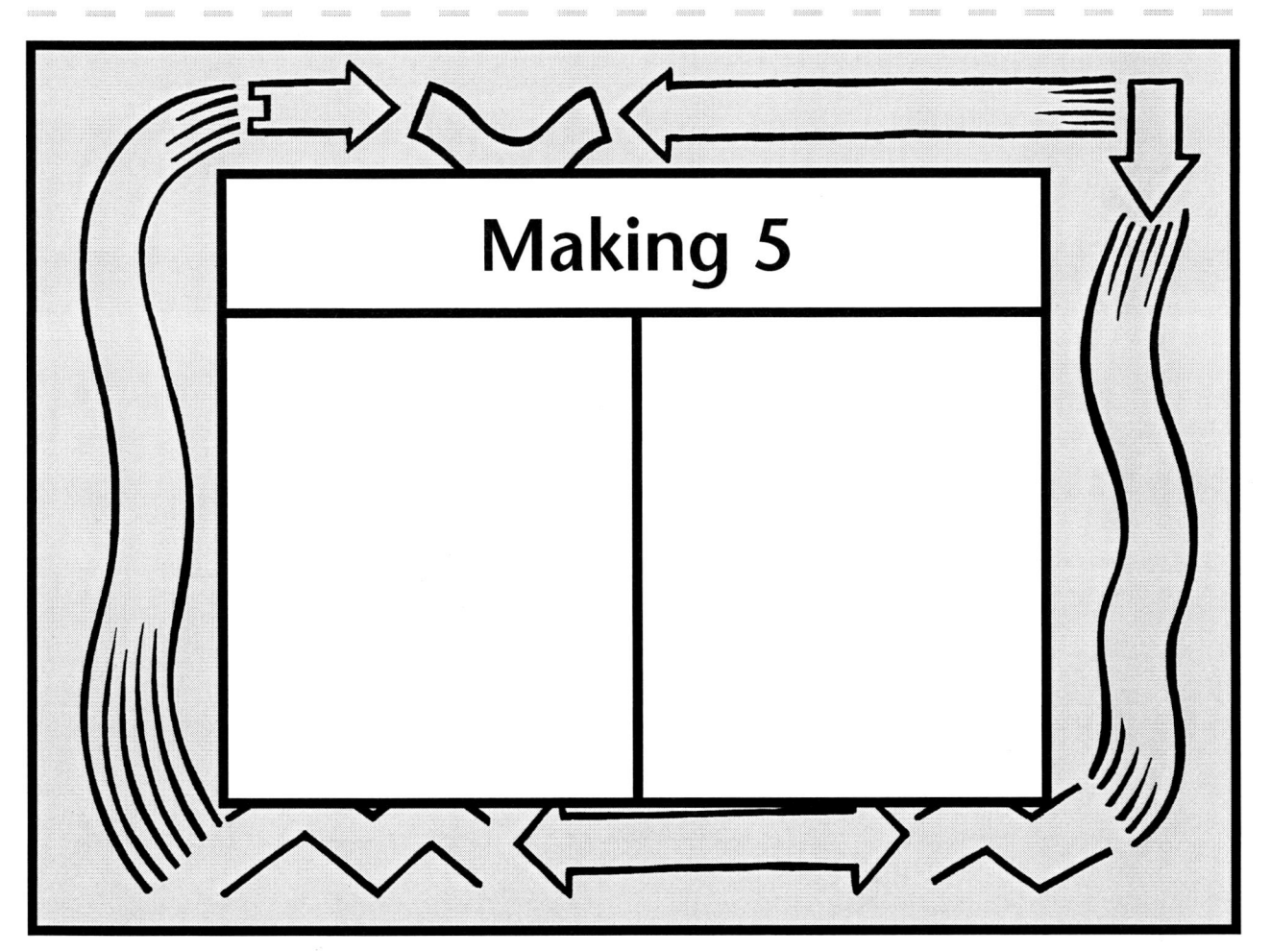

Making 5

Making 5

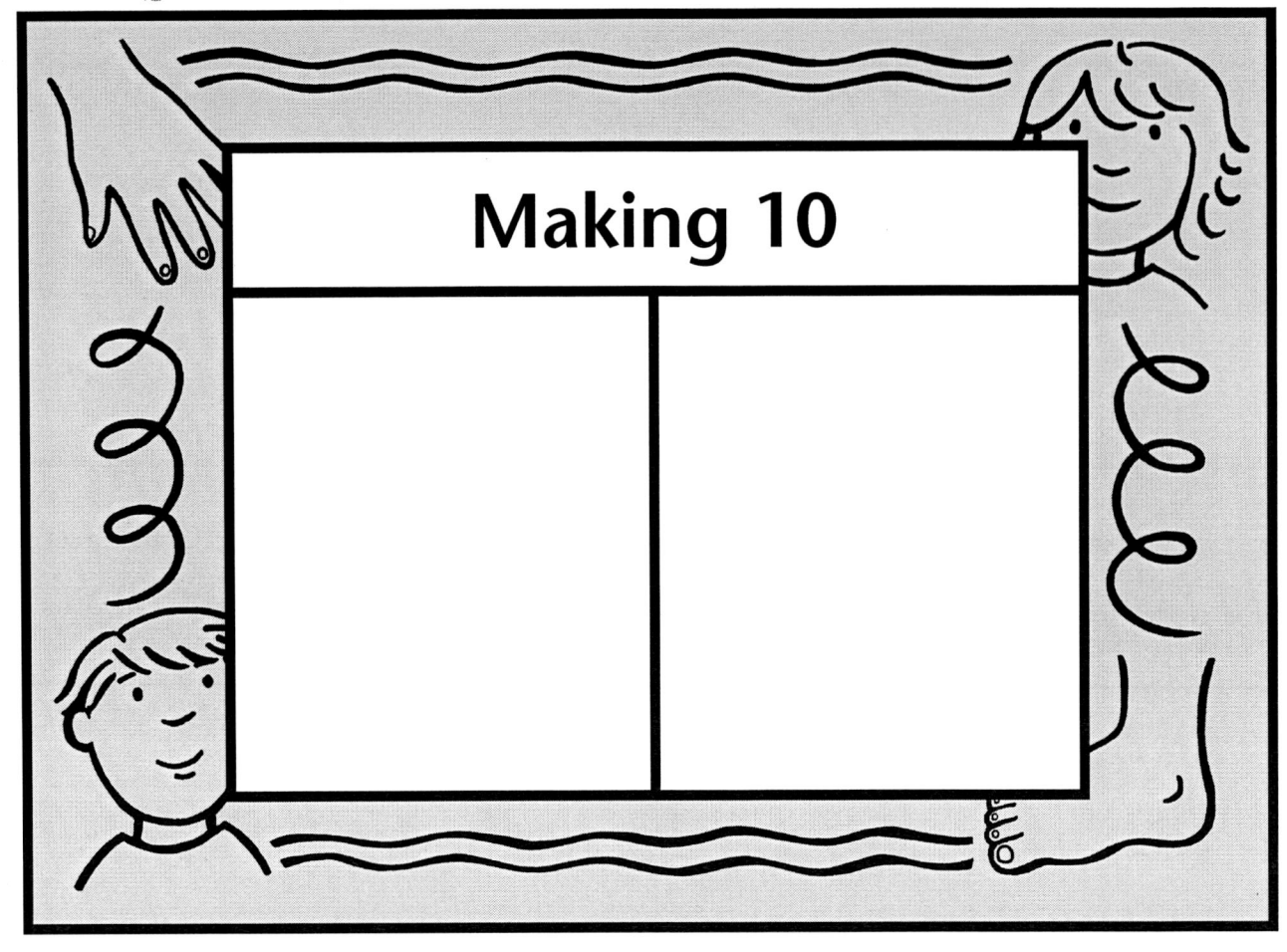

Make it (game boards)

Making 10

Making 10

Make it (game boards)

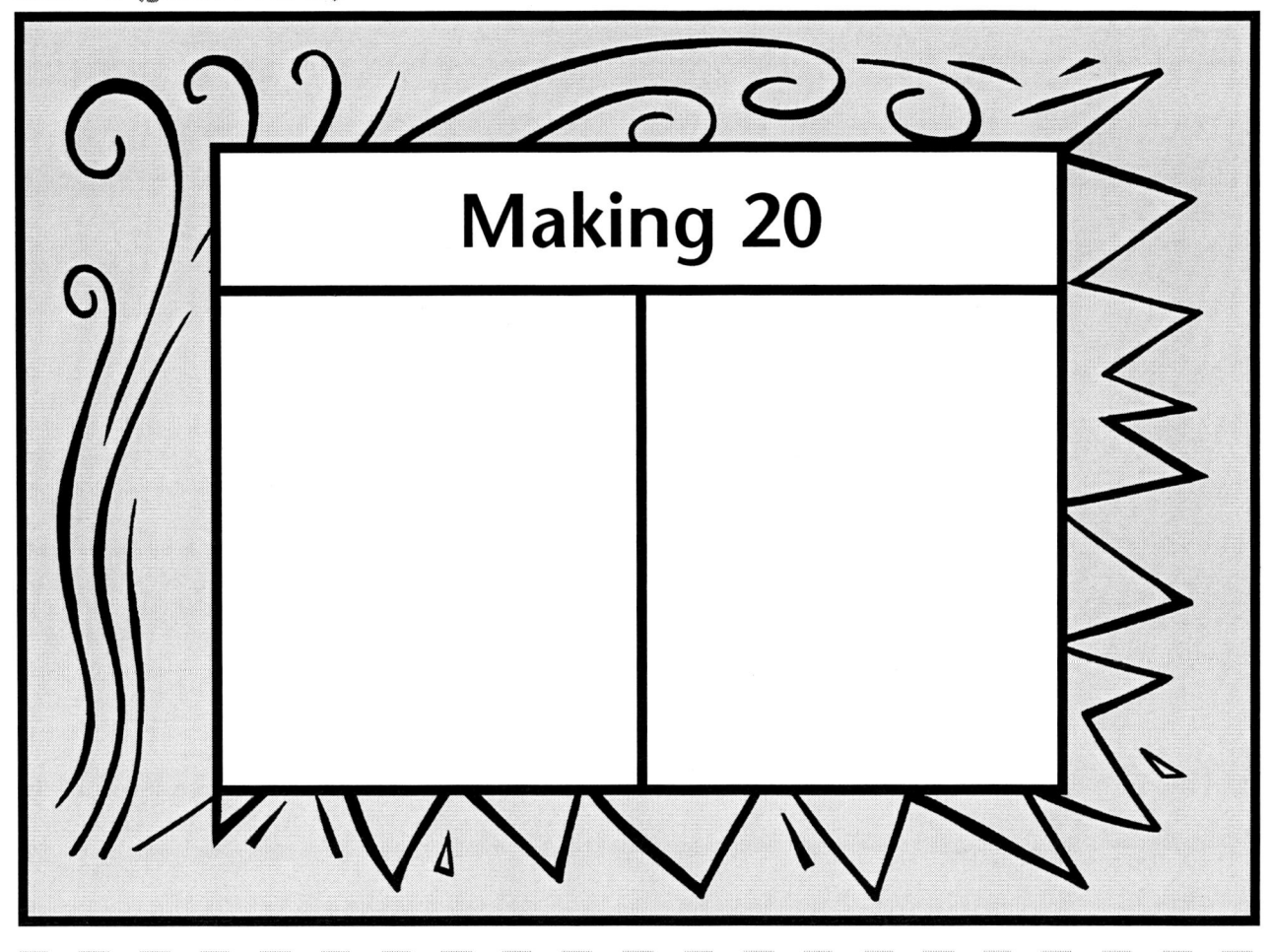

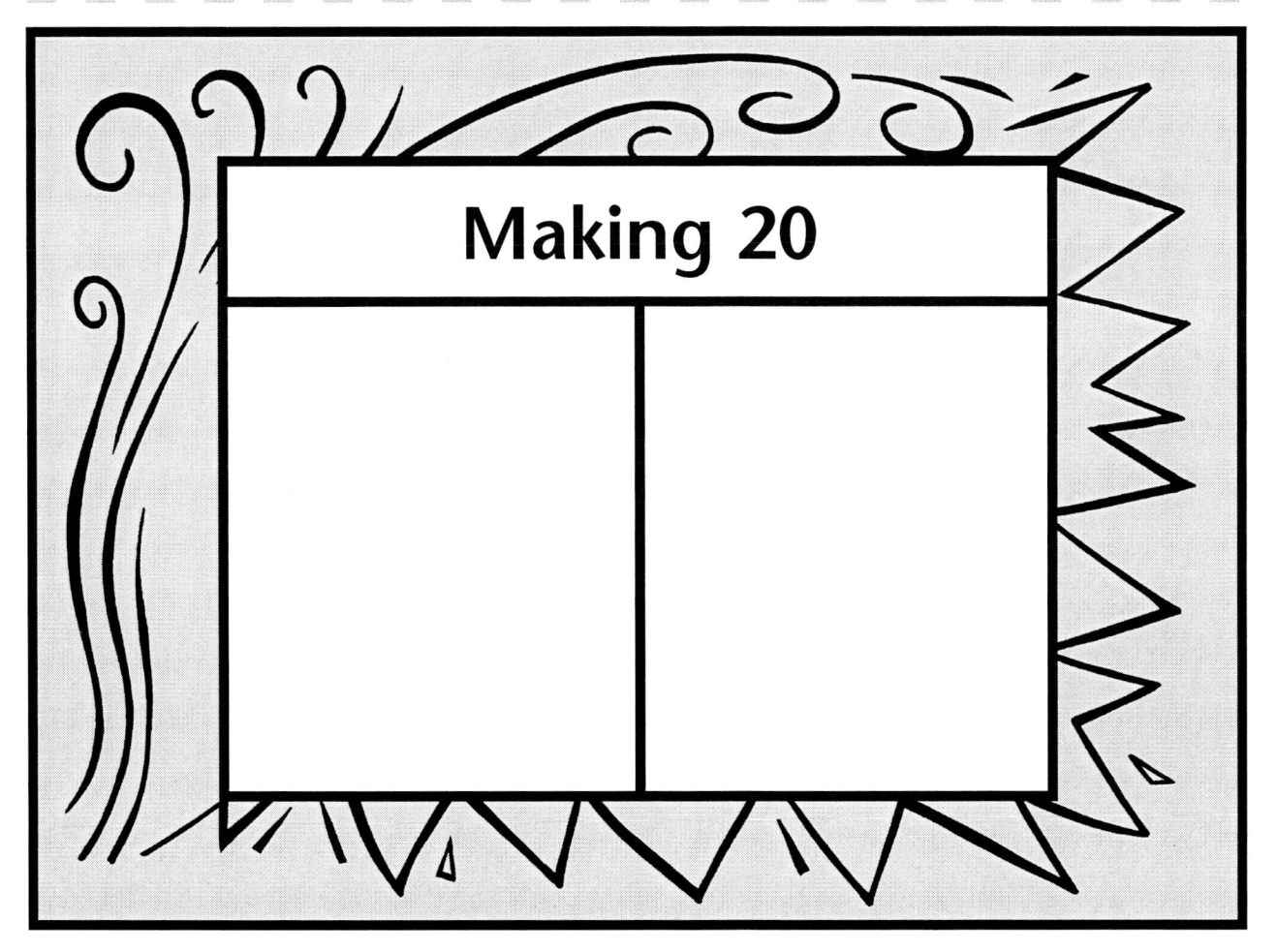

Making 20

Making 20